SO I PUBLISHED A MAGAZINE...

CONVERSATIONS WITH INDEPENDENT PUBLISHERS FROM AROUND THE GLOBE

by
Lorraine Phillips

360 Books
Atlanta, GA

Author: Lorraine Phillips
Editor: Marilyn Burkley
Publishing consultant: Angelicah Rivers
Cover and interior design: Lorraine Phillips
Web: soipublishedamag.com

ISBN-10: 0-9889535-6-0
ISBN-13: 978-0-9889535-6-7

LCCN: 2015921298
Library of Congress subject headings:
1. Magazine publishing.
2. Periodicals—Publishing—United States.

Published by:
360 Books, LLC
PO Box 105603, #22430
Atlanta, GA 30348-5603
Web: 3sixtybooks.com

First Printing
Printed in the United States of America

In loving memory of my dear brother, Leon Phillips.
You will always be one of the biggest dreamers I've ever known.
22 September 1983 – 29 December 2014

Acknowledgments

Thank you to all those who continue to keep me encouraged: Veronica Phillips-Holly, Lady Cherry Igbinedion, Henrietta Girard, Victoria Girard, Barbara Niles, Kimberly Perdue-Sims, Sylvia Copeland, and Sharon Sylvester (who I'd also like to thank for my awesome author pic).

Thanks to all the publishers who gave so generously of their time and for the amazing imagery they so kindly provided: Johanna Agerman Ross, Michael Brooke, David Hershkovits, Charles Hively, David Jenkins, George Macdonald, Helen Martin, Laurence Ng, Ken Olling, Rob Orchard, Rosa Park, Alexander Scholz, Alice Snape, Agata Stoinska, Andre Torres, and Simon Wood.

And lastly, a special thanks to my amazing publishing consultant, Angelicah Rivers. I can't wait till this world gets to see all that you have to offer.

Table of Contents

INTRO

On initial consultations with start-up magazines, right off the bat I'll get questions like:

- What do I need to start a magazine?
- How long will it take for me to put an issue together?
- How much is it going to cost?
- What's the average budget for a start-up magazine?
- How soon can I expect to see a profit?

These are questions that I'm unable to answer without delving further into the specifics of that particular publication, with answers to questions like:

- How much do you know about magazine publishing?
- What's your level of expertise with the subject matter?
- What are your goals for the magazine?
- What's the editorial philosophy behind it?
- Do you have a team, and how big is it?
- How experienced are they?
- Do you plan on recruiting outside help?
- How many pages do you expect the magazine to be?
- How many issues do you plan to publish a year?
- How (and where) will you gather content?
- Do you currently have a social media presence?
- Who's your target audience and how do you plan on marketing to them?
- Do you have any idea which advertisers would be appropriate for your audience, and why?
- What competition do you have and how are you going to be different or better? What's your particular spin on the subject matter?

And so on and so forth—you get the picture. But out of all that came the idea for this book. After all, why not sit down with sixteen independent publishers from around the globe and have honest, candid conversations about what it really takes to start and run a magazine? My intention was not only to provide inspiration for those considering the journey, but also information and insight into the magazine world from publishers who are already in the trenches. I wanted to do it in a way that would allow readers to learn directly from their experience, whether good, bad, or indifferent—and I believe that's what you have now in your hands.

I wanted to select a variety of magazines from "cool" categories (or at least my definition of cool) that have been publishing for various lengths of time and that appear primarily as print publications with the possibility of web or digital counterparts. For good measure, I also decided to include an award-winning digital-only publication (by the name of *Katachi*), just so we could take a look at what that business model looks like in comparison to print.

As you will see, there are many ways to skin a cat, and each publisher will serve to offer a different method or perspective on how to both start and run a magazine. The *only* thing these publishers have in common is their passion for what they do and the fact that they are all indeed independent. As I scoured the web for a concrete definition of what an independent magazine actually is, the description I liked best came from Clive J. on Yahoo! Answers who said, "An independent magazine is a magazine that is not published by a large publishing company and whose editorial policy is dictated by its editor and no one else." Perfect! That's exactly what you want to do (or be), so I got to hunting and this is what I found.

Lorraine Phillips

blw

hold your breath / issue one coming soon / pre blow / limited edition / ten euro

BLOW

AGATA STOINSKA

Magazine name: *Blow*
Founder and executive editor: Agata Stoinska
Year founded: 2010
Tagline: Large format international publication for contemporary photography
Editorial mission: Each issue follows a different theme and acts as a handheld exhibition for some of the best photographers around the world
Location: Dublin, Ireland
Website: blowphoto.com
Format: Print only
Issues per year: Four
Language: English
Reach: Worldwide
Available: Website, digital newsstands, galleries, art spaces, and cafés
Circulation: 3,000
Price per issue: £23.57 (approx. $32 USD)
One-year subscription: £46.89 (approx. $80 USD)
Size of in-house team: Seven part-time

Lorraine: Agata, please kindly tell me a little bit about yourself.
Agata: I'm a professional photographer who's also an architect. Although somewhat of a weird combination, I find that having the two allows me to be a bit more business-minded than the average photographer.

Why did you decide to launch a magazine?
The reason was that as a professional photographer my work has been published in numerous Irish fashion magazines, but I also do loads of private work as well. I like doing professional photography and it's the way to make money, but there wasn't a platform here in Ireland where I could get to show my private projects. I knew that a lot of my colleagues were in the same position, where they too didn't have a platform to show off their private work unless they did something like organize an exhibition or print their own book—which, although quite popular at the moment, wasn't the case

four years ago when I first set up the magazine. So the reason for the magazine was to create a platform that would allow photographers to show their personal projects in a respectable way. It was supposed to just be a quick exercise for Ireland, but I soon found out there was an international need for it as well.

Did you do any market research prior to launching your magazine, or did you just discuss the idea with other photographers and get some feedback from them? How did that all happen?
We were very naive and optimistic when we started the publication, so I'm delighted that I didn't do the proper market research because it would have scared me. Knowing what I know now, I would have never done it [laughs]. If I knew how much work and money you have to invest in your own publication, it would have taken me much longer to launch and I definitely would never have managed to convince

anyone to print such a high quality, large format publication—because financially it just doesn't work. But because we were coming from the perspective of giving photographers the best possible platform to show their work in the biggest format possible, we didn't even consider the numbers.

We started with the A3 format, but it wouldn't fit on the shelves. As an architect I should have known better, because magazine shelves have particular measurements, and as a result we ended up having to make the magazine slightly shorter. We still print on the big sheets and then we have to crop them down—although not the smartest way to do it, we stubbornly want to stick with the quality we have. We don't want to give up on this because we're focused on building a strong brand. We believe the other projects that are connected with *Blow*'s brand will help to bring us financial sustainability in the long run.

How did you fund your first issue?
With my blood [laughs].

[Laughs] I love it. That's a great answer.
I was so enthusiastic about the whole idea. I had it in my mind for months, if not years. On a visit to Poland, I was sitting in a random coffee shop waiting for my friend and flicked through some magazines that were sitting on the table. There was a large format publication called *Między Nami* (which means "between us") that was actually published by the coffee shop, and in that particular issue happened to be a

photographer whose work had been shown at the same exhibition as mine previously in the States. I was like, "Oh my, this looks absolutely beautiful here. This is exactly the way that work should be presented."

I thought it would be amazing to publish something similar in Ireland and create a platform where others could get to show their work. When I got back to Ireland I was so excited about the whole idea that I managed to convince a few people to work on it with me. As I said, we never really thought about the financial side of things because we just wanted to do the project. It was a one-off thing, everyone was working for free, so I had to cover the cost of printing from my own pocket, which turned out to be huge, but our thinking was, "Okay, when we sell the magazine that will give us enough to cover the costs."

We naively set the price to ten euros, which doesn't cover the cost of anything really, but we wanted to price it cheaply enough so that students could afford to buy it. As it turned out, the students couldn't even afford the ten euros and were hoping that the magazine was available for free. For people who had money ten euros was nothing, but we really priced it that low just to make it accessible to all.

I managed to fully sponsor the first issue myself because there were no other costs involved, just printing and delivering it to the stores. Although the costs were kind of huge, when you do your own private projects you are quite happy to invest in them no matter what it takes, so it wasn't a big issue for me. I only hoped that we'd sell enough to where at least part of the money would come back. I never dreamed that we'd be printing *Blow* three times a year with distribution around the world. That's a completely different story—the costs are huge.

How did you come up with the name *Blow*?
It started with a movie called *Blow-Up*, which is about a fashion photographer based in London and was directed by Michelangelo Antonioni. Also, as photographers we're always saying things like, "I'd like my picture blown up for the page," so we constantly use the word "blow." We had originally planned to start out on A4 size paper, but we were like, "No, no, no, let's blow it up to A3." All along I kept saying, "What's the name for it? What's the name?" and we just kept going back to *Blow*.

So how are you different from other magazines out there? What sets your magazine apart from others in the same space, whether it's print, blog, or digital? You have all these photographic-type websites now—how is your magazine different?
To be honest, I find it extremely different. When we were nominated to the Lucie Awards we were nominated along with publications like *Aperture*, *British Journal of Photography*, and *Blind Spot*. This year there was another publication called *Der Greif*, which is a German publication, and they would probably be the closest to what we do. The thing about *Blow*, however, is that we're not really a magazine,

we're like a handheld exhibition. We select the work *very* carefully. The editing process is long and intense. We have long discussions and go back and forth constantly.

The vision is basically to create an exhibition experience with our magazine. It is our intention that each image evoke some kind of emotion from the viewer, and it's very important to us that when you get an edition of *Blow*, you sit comfortably to view your "private collection" at home. You're not disturbed by advertisements, neither are you disturbed by information on how to take good photographs—it's purely visual and gives you a taste of what's going on in the photography world. If something catches your heart, then you can begin to do research by going to the photographer's website and finding out if he or she has an exhibition. The publication just gives you the headspace to appreciate art and to appreciate photography—to stop for just a second, not be disturbed by anything around you, and solely focus on the magazine.

Do you primarily select the content?
Oh no, I collaborate. The content is very subjective, so I have others who work on the publication with me. Loads of people send in submissions, plus we go to portfolio reviews and different festivals so we can view other people's work, which helps us to understand and put some of the images into context. Sometimes the images we didn't like at first become our favorites after hearing the full story behind them.

I work closest with our photo editor, Monika Chmielarz, she has an excellent eye. She carries out loads of research but has completely different taste from mine, which is great because the two of us have to convince each other which is the best picture. We never include pictures that we are both not happy with. The collaboration is great, because it's no longer just about me in terms of the publication. At the beginning I created it to show my work as well, but now I don't care about that side of things because I so enjoy promoting the work of others. I take much inspiration from it.

Who is the magazine aimed at and what does your audience look like? Who buys *Blow*?
It's people who are generally interested in design, who enjoy beautiful objects. It's also for those who enjoy collecting photography—so art collectors, students of photography, and just pure photography lovers—but it's more about people who love design and love having beautiful things around them.

It has to be people that can appreciate it as well, because in terms of photography our publication is pretty difficult. It's not the "easy" type of photography, which means it's not for everyone. Most photography clubs would be interested in, say, pictures of birds or flowers and that type of thing, but our attitude is a bit (I hope) more sophisticated, elegant, and clean—and raises questions. So when you look through the magazine, even if you don't like an image, you have to ask yourself why it's there.

If it's there, there must be a reason for it. It's there because it somehow relates to the others or says something more. So that's our audience as well, those who are seeking something more out of photography.

Interesting. So starting out, how did you attract readers? What did you do online and offline? Was there a launch party? Did you use social media? Did you send out an email blast?
What happened was that in the same week that we published the magazine, PhotoIreland (the Irish photography festival) launched its first edition too. So we organized a big party in the studio that we're based in, called D-Light Studios. It's a studio I started a good few years back and it's basically a massive warehouse with different studios inside.

As we already had a big base and already had the idea for an exhibition, we decided that we would launch *Blow* within that exhibition. PhotoIreland helped as well, they needed support as a new up-and-coming festival while we needed support as an up-and-coming publication. So it all took place in the same week.

But yes, there were loads of emails, setting up of Facebook, letting all my contacts know what was going on—using all my private as well as professional relationships. The big thing was contacting all the photographers I knew from around the world, asking them to support the publication by promoting it on their websites or through their social media channels, and they were very helpful to us in that way.

We try to maintain relationships with the photographers who we feature and always send the publication out to the galleries that represent them. This works well, because then the galleries will want to publish other photographers, which results in them sending us more work, and at the same time they promote the magazine because they want people to see the work of the different artists they represent around the world.

What about distribution?
It's important to find the right distributor to work with, which is not the easiest thing to do because we're such a niche publication. So we need to focus on a distributor who is willing to spend their time on promoting a publication that is really not that easy to sell.

At the moment, we're selling at the price of twenty-five euros, so it's not the cheapest publication either, but for what you're getting, it's very cheap—it just depends on how you look at it. We distribute the magazine ourselves throughout Ireland in the different photography shops and galleries here. We have a UK distributor called Central Books and they take care of our distribution in Europe. Then we have a couple of smaller distributors in New York, for example, who take just a small number of copies but place them in the right locations. We always try to check those locations to see how they're doing and if the magazine is selling well.

Also, when we're traveling around the world we always make sure to check the cities we're in to see if we can find any nice bookshops or galleries or anything along those lines and ask them to promote the magazine there. We ask our photographers where they normally buy magazines and books, and we also sell them during festivals. So we travel around the world with it, and that's usually where we make our sales, through the festivals, and then that follows through to sales online.

As far as the magazine goes, how many people do you have working full-time with you?
It's difficult to say because as there's no money involved, it's not really a full-time thing for any of us. There's about seven of us, plus a couple of interns, but everyone who works on the magazine also does something else as well. For example, I do my photography. I'm the owner of the studio, but fortunately I have a very good manager in the studio so I don't really need to be there as often as I used to. Then I recently started a new online fashion magazine called *maven46*. It's purely online, not printed, fully shoppable, and hopefully a moneymaker [laughs]. So that's what I'm working on too, and then of course there's *Blow*. So my week is split—let's say Mondays I have for my photography, Tuesdays and Thursdays are for *maven46*. Then half of Monday and full Fridays for *Blow*, and then Wednesdays for

kimberly witham / age: 43 / nationality: american / currently based: new jersey, usa / witham's work is strongly influenced by natural history displays, or dioramas, cabinets of curiosity and still life compositions. her work reflects man's attempt to categorize, comprehend and ultimately control the natural world. witham finds abundant road kill on her drive to work and, unlike other naturalists who dried, pickled or mounted their specimens, she has preserved them through photography. the clean white backgrounds signify both the clinical eye of science and suburban perfection and domesticity.

something else. I juggle as needed, but that's basically how I work.

What do you find the most challenging part of running a magazine?
Finding the money, that's the most challenging.

You mean to print each issue?
Yes, to sponsor each issue, that's very challenging. Also, even though we have a good number of people working on the magazine, as I said, none of them are full-time, and that's a big challenge because we are extremely focused and very stressed right before going to print, giving it 110 percent. Once the issue finally comes out, we're completely exhausted and need to take a break, but in the real world we would have to pick straight back up, so it's a challenge to constantly remain alert, focused, and optimistic about it all the time.

What's the most rewarding part? What makes you feel good? Is it the awards, your readers, personal emails?
Readers and photographers. The biggest reward for us is when we get replies from well-established photographers. Sometimes they've never even heard of us when we approach them or they're not really sure who we are and why we want a particular set of pictures. He or she may have just released a new collection and would prefer to promote those instead. But as we're so strict with our choices, we tell them we will only take the ones that we've selected, but would be happy to promote the others through our social media or even add them to our

newsletter. Sometimes the photographer will take the attitude of, "Yes, but you're not even paying me, so what's this?" [laughs].

But we do promote our photographers, we care about their work. We send it to various museums, galleries, art collectors—so in this way we promote them big-time. A few of them—based on the fact that they show their work next to big names that are published in our magazine—get great reviews and maybe even commissions on the back of that. So it's great, we almost work like their agent as we get to promote them. The best reward I think is a few weeks later after they receive the magazine and the email comes back saying, "I never realized that this was so beautiful. It's amazing. I'm so proud to be involved." And that makes us really, really happy.

Then when we go to festivals, people come up and say, for instance, "Can you sign this for me somewhere?" Or "Do you have issue four, that's the only one I'm missing from the collection?" At the moment we stamp every copy, so they are all individually numbered. There are people collecting particular numbers of each issue, so that's another nice thing when we get the emails to make sure that a certain reader's issue number is this and this. When we get personal emails from photographers and readers, that's the most rewarding.

We also carry out fundraisers. The last issue was sponsored solely by our readers, and to see people sending money to support us—and some we knew for sure couldn't afford it, so we wrote back saying, "Do you realize that there's an extra zero on here? We're just making sure that you want to put this money towards the magazine." To hear them say, "Yeah, we want to support you, we believe in you, and this is the least we can do,"—it's truly amazing.

Are these individuals or companies?
Individuals. There were a good few galleries that supported us, and that was good to see. But in the end it was just amazing to see the long list of people who just believed in us, which makes us know that what we do is needed and appreciated.

You said that the magazine is not currently profitable—what other activities do you carry out under the magazine's name (events, shows, annuals, etc.) that contribute to the bottom line?
We make money through projects that are related to *Blow*, like editing and printing commissioned books or catalogues for exhibitions. We're actually going to print on Tuesday with a special edition of *Blow* for the Southeast Museum of Photography in Florida. That's a commissioned job, so this way we'll get funding for the next issue. As I mentioned, we also carry out fundraisers. Our last issue was funded by our readers or people who wanted to be able to buy the next issue in advance. It hadn't been printed yet, but as they ordered up-front, it gave us a nice way to collect the money and use it towards the print costs. All these types of things help to keep our publication going.

What factors do you think contribute to the success of a magazine in general?
It really depends how you look at it, because commercially I'd probably be the last person to answer that question, unfortunately [laughs]. But I would say, based on the other publication I'm working on, *maven46*, which is a commercial project, that it's proper market research to know that you have an audience and that they will buy. Mind you, this goes for every product you put on the market, not just for publications.

Okay, so you think adequate market research is what can help?
Yes. Also, if you asked me how to build a successful brand, I would say being consistent and being true to your values, having respect for your readers, not cutting corners, and just doing your work 110 percent. I really believe in that. For me, *Blow* is this perfect baby who I don't want to spoil, I just want to raise it as 100 percent beautiful. I will always make time for it and I will never reduce the quality. If I ever have to stop, I will just stop. I hope that never happens, but I refuse to drop the quality in any way. I hope it is going to be a very, very strong brand doing commissioned projects that will help to keep the publication alive, because I truly believe in it. I have a very good team of people who believe in it as well. They are all sensitive, special, and talented people.

I can really see your genuine passion for the publication and for photography. But let me ask, what do you think contributes to the failure of a magazine? "Failure" is a subjective

word, but for readers who may be starting out and need to look out for certain things— if you say that proper market research can help a publication succeed, do you think that a lack of research can contribute to failure or are there other factors involved as well?

Yes, a lack of research can be a big problem, and also if you don't have a clear vision you can end up doing a little bit of this and a little bit of that. It's important to test the market and you may have to tweak your publication a bit. Like in our situation, it was cropping down the size of the magazine to fit the shelves. We've also changed the packaging, we made it nicer and more secure for postage. These are the types of things that you may need to change.

In terms of content, if you're not clear about what your publication is about, that can be very confusing for a reader. There are a few publications I would buy when traveling around the world because I'd be intrigued by the cover. I'd look at the first few pages and be like, "Oh yes, this looks very interesting," and take it on the plane with me. But once I looked through, I'd be like, "I'm not really sure what this magazine is about or who it's aimed at," and it just doesn't make me feel like I'd want to subscribe or even buy another issue.

What types of skills or disciplines do you think are important for magazine publishers to have today? If I came up to you and said I wanted to publish a magazine, what would you say is important for me to know or do?

That again is a tricky question, because I myself didn't have the skills that would probably be required on paper. But based on my experience, I would say first of all have a clear vision. The other thing is management skills so you can get together a group of people who have the best possible skills for the different parts of your magazine—the editor, the writer, the copywriter, the graphic designer, a good printer. You have to be the person who joins all the dots and makes it work so that everyone can follow the schedule and fulfill the big vision of the magazine. I mean, you get to where you have to write a business plan, and that's another creative thing—to write a plan. People are usually scared of writing one, and I must admit it's not my favorite thing to do in the world.

Oh, so you've written one?

Yeah, yeah. I didn't write it at the very beginning, because at the beginning it was just an art project, it wasn't supposed to be a business—as far as I was concerned it was going to be a one-off thing. But as I started applying for different grants and loans, I had to write a business plan. It helps you to really focus. You have to do things like predict trends and write out your strengths, weaknesses, opportunities, and threats.

Yes, the acronym is SWOT.

Exactly, and then you put everything on a time scale, which allows you to be a little bit bold, because you can start asking yourself where you'd like to see yourself or the magazine in

ten years time and you can have this big vision. Then you try to break it down and figure out the steps you can take to get there and start building from there.

How many years into the future does your business plan go? I think you might be the second or third publisher I've interviewed who's actually written one.

Well, a business plan is something you have to hatch just to keep you focused. You can go back and say, "Oh, actually I've done this already, which I thought I was going to do next year," which is great, or you can say, "Oh no, I don't think this thing is ever going to work, I should drop it." So then you start rewriting your plan, but it's like your plan for life and you just change it depending on your circumstances or according to things that happen. You have to constantly adapt it.

How often do you find yourself revisiting your plan, say during the year? Is it every three months or so that you might take a look through and reevaluate?

Well, normally we have weekly meetings or at least every second week, just to see where we are with different things and to decide what's coming up next. And about once a month we'll summarize the situation as far as what's going on—like we need to check if the invoices are sent, or find out how many magazines we still have in the stores and those types of things. When is the next issue coming? When is the next festival? Who's going to the festival? How much is it going to cost? Where are we going to get the money? So that's typically what we discuss every month. Then for me, I make myself a list of my big goals and put in the smaller steps that will allow me to get there. And every now and again, maybe every three months or so, I look at the big goals to see if they've changed. Maybe I've lost my focus, or maybe I've forgotten about something that I need to go back and do. As an entrepreneur you can't constantly carry ideas around in your head, so I think it's important to take the time to put them on paper and be disciplined enough to occasionally review and run through them.

Agata, what last message of wisdom or inspiration do you have for someone who may be considering launching their own publication?

The first thing I'd say is to take a deep breath and ask yourself do you really want this. Is there a hidden agenda? Do you think you'll make loads of money? Do you think you'll become famous? Or is it something that you really want from your heart?

For any publication or project you decide to start, you really have to know deep in your heart that it's something you love and are happy to put quite a bit of money and time into. Also, do you have the people that will work together on it with you? Because you can't do it on your own, you have to have a great team of people. It doesn't need to be huge, but just two people will help you stay balanced and focused. When your energy is low, their energy might be high or vice versa, which will help you keep it together. Working with others will also help you see mistakes earlier on, as you can bounce ideas around and get to see things from different perspectives. Also, if you surround yourself with a set of creative people they'll help you come up with new ideas too. So don't do it on your own but instead be a leader.

I think that's great advice. And lastly, is there anything you would like to add or wish I had asked?
Well, in terms of photography publications, I'd like to make this statement to all photographers. If they'd like to be featured in a publication like ours (or any other for that matter) buy the publication to support it, and before submitting your work, check what the publication is about so you're not wasting your time or theirs by just sending material that's not appropriate for that particular publication. As much as we respect photographers and their work, we ask that they do the same in return. If we all start supporting each other, it will help to promote everything and keep niche publications like ours alive.

C E R E A L

Travel & Lifestyle VOL. 1

2

CEREAL

ROSA PARK

Magazine name: *Cereal*
Founder and editor: Rosa Park
Year founded: 2013
Tagline: Travel and lifestyle
Editorial mission: To bring interesting content to travel under the realm of lifestyle
Location: Bristol, UK
Website: readcereal.com
Format: Print only
Issues per year: Four
Language: English
Reach: UK
Available: Website, digital newsstands, and newsstands
Circulation: 25,000
Price per issue: £10 (approx. $15 USD)
One-year subscription: £40 (approx. $60 USD)
Size of in-house team: Two full-time and two part-time

Lorraine: Rosa, can you tell me a little about what you were doing before you launched your magazine?
Rosa: I started out in fashion and beauty marketing in New York, and then pursued my master's degree in English literature. Right before I launched my magazine I was working for a local title in Bath, here in the UK.

What made you decide to start a publication?
I suppose, like most other independent publishers, you love magazines and you feel like you can create your own so you give it a go.

Did you do any market research or create a business plan prior to launching?
It's a wise and cautious thing to do and I probably should have, but I did not. Unfortunately, most editors are not business people per se.

Yes, as I'm finding out. How did you select your magazine's name?

It's actually an inside joke between my business partner and me, a silly story really. Basically, I think a name becomes completely neutralized after a while because you just accept it at face value. You don't really wonder why a brand is a certain name; it's never something I think about. Maybe other people do, but I don't. I don't wonder why Apple is called Apple (although I know why, because I read Steve Job's biography). It's quite a random name for a computer company, but I never for one second wondered why.

So you were thinking along those same lines when you selected *Cereal* as the title for your magazine?
Yes, plus every single name in the world was pretty much taken at the time [laughs]. Anything that is remotely related to travel or another title or brand already exists, so I think at this point in the game you just pick something that is personal to you and works.

How has it worked for you? It's a word that people use almost every day, so it should be quite easy for them to remember.
Yes, it's good that people don't forget it. In terms of names, I think the simpler the better. With *Cereal* there's no opportunity for misinterpretation, misspelling, or anything like that. I mean everything about the magazine is very pared back and simple, so the name is also a reflection of that.

How did you initially fund your magazine?
I had a private investment.

Did you create a proposal for an outside investor or was it something more on a personal level?
I got a private investment from somebody I knew personally, so it was definitely much more informal than going to an outside investor that I didn't have a prior relationship with.

What was your initial vision for the magazine?
I just wanted to create a title that talked about travel in a way that felt accessible to my peers and me.

Are you saying that there was nothing out there that was speaking to you at the time?
I would say specifically in the travel market, yes, not so much.

Your magazine and website have a very unified, distinct, clean look and feel about them. They strongly represent and effectively communicate your brand, giving an accurate depiction of what it's all about. How were you able to conceptualize and communicate your vision so well?
I think it just comes down to taste really. It's what my creative director and I like. Taste is tricky because it's obviously very subjective and it evolves over time. I mean it can, depending on your personality, but I think the aesthetics of our publication is very much in line with the things I like. If you came over to my apartment, you would see the influences there. Or to trace it back even further, if you were to visit my parent's home, you can see how clean and minimalist it is, so I think it's something I grew up with—that kind of aesthetic sensibility. When I was trying to figure out the visual direction of our title with our creative director, it came very naturally because we already knew what we both liked and it feels natural to pursue what's most comfortable to you.

That makes total sense. And I understand that *Cereal* has had some rave reviews and even awards. Can you tell me some more about that?
I don't really know because I don't pay much attention to that side of things. Not because I don't think it's important, it's just not something that really comes up in my day-to-day. If people have written rave reviews about us, then I'm very, very flattered and honored and obviously that's fantastic because that means that we are finding readers who appreciate what we do. In terms of awards, I don't think that we've

won many [laughs]. Recently we were awarded something from a paper merchant here in the UK, but we never submit our title for awards. With most award ceremonies you have to submit yourself, and that's very counter-intuitive to what we do. I don't think that you should rate yourself, I feel that it's for others to judge.

Yes, and they are. What would you say sets you apart from others who are in the same space, whether it's print, blog or digital?
Just my own opinions really, because no two people have the exact same opinions. It can be simple but it's still ultimately distinct because no two people are alike, so I think that's really our point of departure. It's just our personal opinions.

And who is the magazine aimed at? What does your audience look like?
When we created the title I often pictured my friends and me because, again, for me it's always about coming back to that familiar territory, so that's who I'm targeting. But who I'm targeting, and whose hands it ends up in, can sometimes be very different.

So how did you attract readers starting out? What did you do online and offline to get the word out? Were you building a following, letting people know about the imminent launch, and taking them along the journey with you?
I think when you're an independent title with limited funding you are pretty much working

with bare bones, so you have a title that you've printed and that you're trying to distribute to the channels you feel are most relevant to your readership. You have to reach out to those particular stores and see if they're willing to take a chance on your mag. Social media is an obvious one because it's free and it's instant and it has the capacity to bring you a very large audience depending on how fast your following grows. So we did all the social media straight off the bat: Facebook, Twitter, Tumblr, Pinterest, and Instagram. The audience has organically grown from there over the past two years.

I noticed that you have quite a huge following online. How have you managed to grow your audience so quickly?
I think a lot of it has to do with just how much quality control you do in terms of the content that you post on social media. I don't know what other magazines do, but for us when we post things on our various channels we take it almost as seriously as what we actually do for our print title. It's definitely not less important. So whatever image or words we put up on social media is a clear reflection of what you'll find in our magazine.

I think quality control has played a factor in our growing numbers and I also think sometimes these things just happen. There isn't a science to it, otherwise everyone would have millions of followers. I think it's just luck, people finding you, word of mouth, and so much of people's quote, unquote *success* has a lot to do with just

luck—I really mean that. Everybody has to work hard—that is not even worth mentioning because it's a given—you have to be talented, you have to have a vision. These are the things that people have to check off the list and then the final boost that you need is just the right timing and a bit of luck.

Do you track any analytics for social media or do you just let it be whatever it happens to be?
We just let it be. I think you miss the point of social media if you start analyzing it and taking it too seriously. At the end of the day I think it's important to just have fun with it.

I noticed on YouTube that a student had created a digital prototype of *Cereal* on the iPad for a class project. Have you seen it yet?
I have not, actually.

It's very beautiful and I think you'd be both honored and impressed. Do you foresee digital in the future for *Cereal*?
I wouldn't rule it out. To be perfectly honest I just haven't seen a digital version of a magazine that I felt was superior to what we have in print right now. If we were to do a digital one, we would want it to offer our readers something that our print magazine does not, and at the moment I haven't come up with a version that can do that in the digital realm. That's not to say that we won't, because something may happen in the future that prompts us to want to go down that road, but yes, I'm not really sure right now—only time will tell.

What can you tell me about your current distribution? You've managed to grow pretty fast and have a lot of visibility whether on the newsstand or in specialty shops. How did that come about?
I think a lot of it had to do with the fact that we handled our distribution in-house for so long. I think a lot of independent titles are doing that now but obviously your mainstream titles don't necessarily do that as they work with huge distribution companies. I wouldn't speak negatively of distribution companies but I will say that no one is going to sell your publication and take care of it better than yourself.

So you're actually on the phone ringing up stores and getting the magazine placed?
In the beginning, yes I was.

And what about now? Have you partnered with any distribution companies?
Yes. Now we have a pretty intricately layered distribution system. Some of it's still handled in-house, but we also work with six different distribution companies because of the different ways that we approach different markets. But every magazine needs to find a system that works best for them depending on where they want to be seen and how fast they want to grow (or not grow). You have to calculate your sell-through, how much is getting recalled, how much is actually selling, and where the magazine is being shown. I think it's hard to say, I don't necessarily have a formula—I think it's a case-by-case scenario from volume to volume.

How many people do you have on your team?
My business partner and me, so that's two full-time staff, and then we have a part-time advertising manager and a part-time sales manager.

How long does it typically take for you to plan and put together an issue?
We come out quarterly, so I would say it's roughly about a month of planning and research, a month of actual creation time, and a month of designing and production.

Can you briefly describe the process from planning the table of contents to completing the final layout? How do you decide on the contents that each issue will contain and the particular theme?
I think that between my creative director and me, we have a constant running list of things we're interested in. We try to have a nice editorial pace and balance in every volume, so we make sure that there's a little bit of everything in there in terms of travel and lifestyle. Then we whittle and distill that list down to chapters because, as you may know, our magazine is actually divided into topic-specific chapters, and once we have that set we travel to those locations to create the content.

I noticed that (at least) three issues of *Cereal* were completely sold out. Do you use that as a gauge to let you know that you need to increase the number of copies that are being printed, maybe for the next issue?

Yes, and we've actually been increasing the number that we print every single issue since we launched.

Wow, that's impressive. What do you find most challenging about running a magazine?
The business side of it. Making the magazine is easy, that's what's the most fun and the reason why people start magazines in the first place, but that's not what's going to sustain your business for the long term—you need to quickly figure out how you're going to make money, pay your bills, pay your contributors, etc., etc.

And what do you find the most rewarding? What really makes you feel good about working on this publication?
I would say that it is two-fold. First, I think the obvious answer—and I'm sure most publishers would say this—is that it's just nice to know that people are appreciating what you've created. At the end of the day, you are one person who's making something and you're not really sure if people are necessarily going to want to read or buy it. So to see people buying the magazine from the stores and to see your circulation grow, that's very motivating. I can imagine that it would be frustrating if you're giving it 500 percent but your sales are not growing, or they're even decreasing. So a very big motivating factor for me is growth, or if not growth, then maintenance.

The second most rewarding and motivating thing for me personally as an editor is the

kind of brands and people I get to work with that I never dreamed of when I first started the magazine.

What factors do you think contribute to the success of a magazine in general?
I don't really know, if I knew that then I'd be a millionaire, right? I don't really know if anyone knows the answer to that one [laughs].

That's one of the reasons why I'm writing this book—I'm trying to find out [laughs].
You can have great advice from people who've experienced all these different things about publishing and there's great wisdom and value in that, but I think for me, when people ask that question it's kind of the usual suspects: you have to have good content, you have to try to make every issue the best it can be—don't rest on your laurels, or get too comfortable. I think that's a big thing for me, constantly striving to be better. Both my business partner and I are quite intense in that regard—we're never quite content, so we're constantly pushing the boundaries of what we can achieve. Also, you have to work really hard. I say this to people and they're like, "Yeah, yeah," and I'm like, "NO, I don't think you understand." I mean my personal life has taken a huge hit in sacrifice since starting the magazine, to the point where I'm sure I've even compromised my health at some points. But what my dad said to me growing up was that you work one hour longer than the next man and you will be that much more successful—so hard work goes a long way.

What factors do you think contribute to a magazine's failure? Do you have any ideas on what readers should be looking out for?
It's actually quite difficult to answer that question because I don't really know the nuts and bolts of why so many magazines are not doing as well and folding. I guess the general assumption is that these magazines are operating on a very archaic model that hasn't really changed or moved with the times. I mean that's an obvious answer that everyone would probably agree on.

Also, there was something a friend said to me that stuck with me, she said, "You know, with even the best magazine, the longest lifespan will be a decade." Because a magazine often represents the zeitgeist and is very much about capturing that moment, I think it's hard for any editor or single magazine to be able to do that forever. That might have a lot to do with why some of the older titles are suffering— they've been around for years and they haven't changed a thing. I mean, it's hard to just up and change something, especially when you're a huge company and you don't have the agility afforded by smaller companies. It's those types of things that can contribute to—I don't want to use the word failure—but the struggle. For me, agility, flexibility, and evolution are three things that are really key to having a successful title in the long term.

Your ad strategy is quite interesting: there was no advertising initially. What made you decide to start including ads later on?

CEREAL

Travel & Lifestyle VOL. **8**

I can't speak on behalf of other titles, but I don't know how one would make a healthy profit without advertising, no matter how many magazines you sell, unless you're actually selling in the millions. If you're traveling to every single place you're covering and expensing the cost of your team, your overheads, your printing costs, it just doesn't work. I thought that for a minute maybe it could, but I think in the long term it just doesn't. There's a reason why advertising exists in magazines.

I understand that you try to ensure that the ads fit in aesthetically with your magazine, even shooting some yourself.

Yes, I think that's something a lot of the newer titles are beginning to do as well because they understand that they've built their title on a very strong sense of aesthetics and you can't just abandon that now that you have advertising—so I think you meet each other halfway. You pick the brands that you feel are in line with what you do, brands that you feel you and your reader would genuinely, happily shop at, and you also have the capacity to design and shoot those ads yourself. So if a brand is receptive to that, it's really lovely because then it seamlessly integrates into our content.

When we made our first foray into advertising, starting earlier this year, we knew that we were going from zero advertising to advertising, and you have to be transitioning into that step-by-step because I don't think anybody appreciates abrupt, abrasive change. I believe in easing your

readership into the process with you, so that you're doing it together almost.

Basically you've decided that you're not going to sell your soul for ads.

Well you know, I would love to say that we're going to be that way [laughs], but you can never say never.

I understand that you have other endeavors that complement the magazine, like offering travel guides for instance.

Yes, we have city guides which exist both online and in print. We've just printed the London run and it's been received quite well, which we're very happy about. We're going into our second print run soon. We're going to roll out four more city guides next year, so by the end of 2015 you will have five printed city guides by *Cereal* in circulation, alongside the title.

We also do a lot of consultancy work and brand direction. That came about pretty organically. I'm sure other titles have experienced the same, where people say, "Hey, I like what you're doing with the magazine, can you do that for us?" So it's nice that we get to work with really great brands.

What skills would you say are crucial for a magazine publisher or editor?

I think you need to have great people skills, because half the battle is trying to convince people that your title is worth advertising in, working for, or partnering with—that definitely helps. But I think that can sometimes be frustrating, because I believe it comes naturally with personality, it's something that's more innate than learned. That's definitely something to bear in mind, whether you have a personality that's outgoing, charming, engaging, and convincing. Actually, I think that's the most important skill—people skills.

What last message of wisdom or inspiration would you like to leave with readers who may be thinking about launching a publication themselves?
Wisdom I have; inspirational words, I'm not sure [laughs].

Well either one will do [laughs].
I've had people ask me for words of advice when they're starting their own magazine, and I don't think this is very inspirational, but it's honest. I tell them, make sure you have the money to start a magazine. I don't think to just have enough for one issue, hoping that that's going to carry you into the second is fine. I would not advise it, because you've no idea what's going to happen after you launch issue one, and you probably don't want to be the title that launched issue one and never got to two. So I think the biggest advice I would give to anyone starting their own magazine is to make sure that you've secured the proper amount of funding that can last you for a significant period of time.

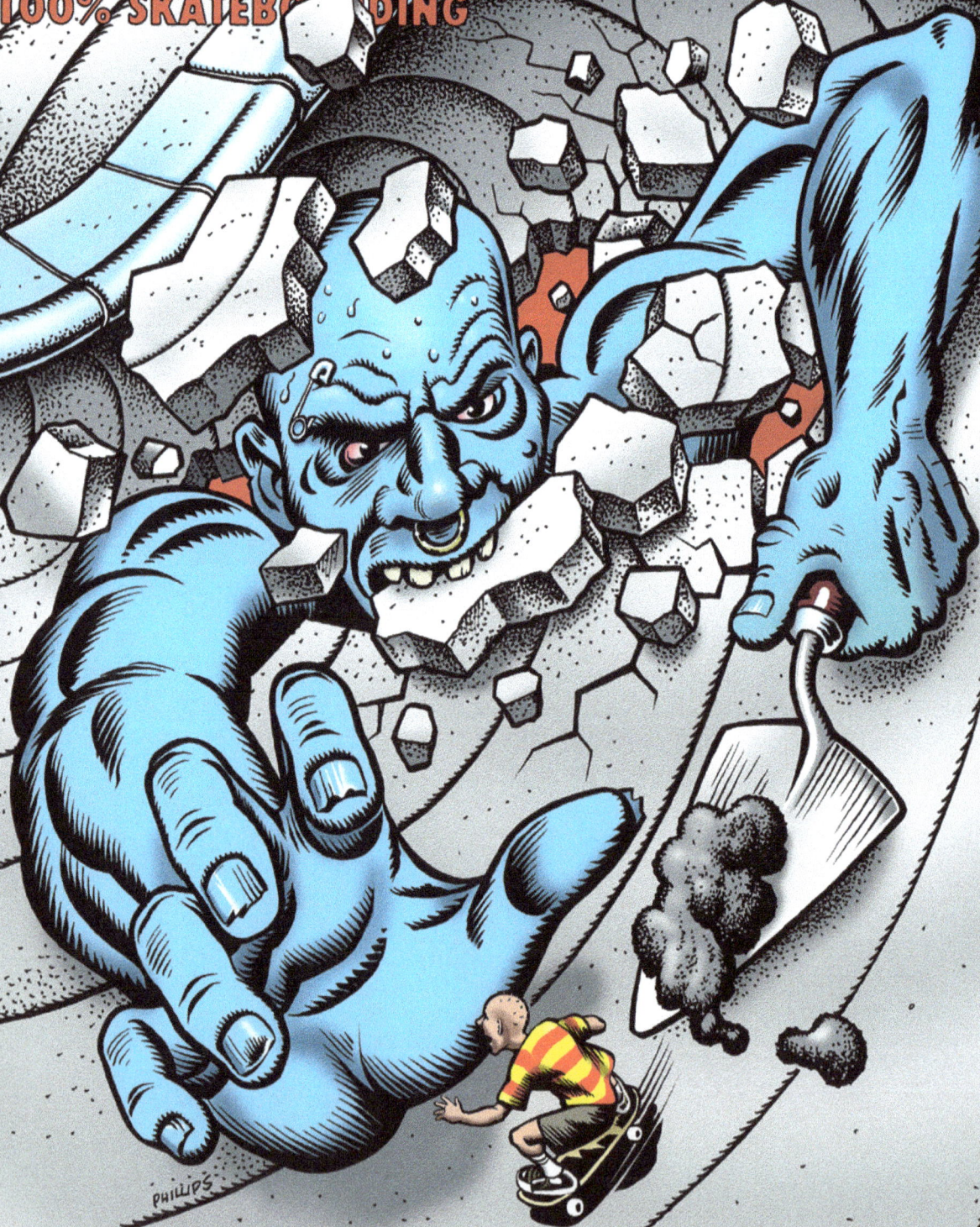

CONCRETE WAVE

MICHAEL BROOKE

Magazine name: *Concrete Wave*
Founder and publisher: Michael Brooke
Year founded: 2002
Tagline: The ride is the reward
Editorial mission: To offer a unique perspective in the world of skateboarding, celebrating all types of riders and terrain
Location: Thornhill, Canada
Website: concretewavemagazine.com
Formats: Print and digital
Issues per year: Six
Language: English
Reach: Worldwide
Available: Website, digital newsstands, app stores, independent skate shops, and events
Circulation: 20,000
Price per issue: $4.95 USD
One-year subscription: $26.00 USD
Size of in-house team: One full-time

Lorraine: Michael, what did you do before you launched your magazine?
Michael: Basically I was a failed Xerox salesman [laughs]. I'm not kidding, I really was.

A failed Xerox salesman?
Yes. I literally was selling these very large photocopiers called Docutechs to book publishers.

Okay.
Come to find out that most book publishers just want to publish their work and print it anywhere they can, so it was a bit of a lost cause to begin with. I managed to bully this guy into meeting me and somewhere during my sales pitch I mentioned that I had a website, and he was like, "Oh really, what's your site about?" So I told him it was on skateboarding. "That's interesting," he said, "We're thinking about doing a book on skateboarding, why don't you put together a little outline for us," so I did. About

a week later I met with him again, showed him my outline, was given an advance, and ended up writing the book.

I jumped the slush pile so to speak, I jumped all the people in line trying to get their books out. Back in 1995 if you had a website it was a big deal—come to think of it, if you had email it was a big deal. And so this little five-dollar-a-month website I owned was the catalyst that brought this whole new world to me. I wrote the book, it sold 42,000 copies and it turned into a TV show over the next four years. Once that was all over I thought to myself, "What can I do now?" I realized that my wife was going out exercising every night and I would need something to do, so I decided to start a magazine on longboarding.

What's the difference between longboarding and skateboarding?

Skateboarding generally consists of males who are usually under the age of eighteen, doing very difficult tricks that are all about flippin', rails and ledges, and all kinds of stuff, but the world of longboarding is a little more soulful, it's a little more creative. It's more like surfing on asphalt, if you will. My original skate experience (I've been skating for over forty years now) was very much like the longboard, just kind of rolling and flowing, but it was something the skate industry wasn't interested in and so they didn't want to promote it. I found the niche, so that's what I decided to do. I just went out there and covered all these guys and wrote about their companies. All of them were very small at the time, but I've watched them progress over the last fifteen years.

You said "surfing on asphalt"—is that where the name *Concrete Wave* came from?
Actually no, I stole it. There was a skateboard park called Concrete Wave. It's probably the greatest name in skateboarding and it's also the name I used for my book.

From the way things progressed for you it doesn't seem that you had the need to create a business plan. It sounds like you just kind of went for it.
I did. But right now I'm at a crossroads in the sense that I may have to bring in a few people. The industry's changed a lot, but up until now I pretty much just muddled through—I didn't know what I was doing. I never went to publishing school, I hadn't done it before, and as I told you, I'm a terrible salesman. I'm the worst salesperson in the world except for one thing, and that is that I can sell an idea. When it comes to selling ideas I'm probably one of the best at it. And I can sell ideas inexpensively too. The first magazine I did cost me fifty dollars in phone calls. I just called people up and said, "Hey remember me, I did the book. Well now I'm putting together a magazine, do you want to be a part of it?"

What was the number of your first print run?
It was 25,000 and consisted of a 16-page piece. I look at it now and just cringe. I had no idea what I was doing, I just did it. Now I hear sums like you need two hundred and fifty thousand, you need one million. I hear crazy, crazy talk but I always laugh because I don't play by those rules and as a skateboarder I suppose that's what happened. Basically, I'm a skateboarder who became a magazine publisher, as opposed to a journalist who became a magazine publisher or a business guy. Looking at it now, my revenues at one point were very high. They're still pretty high but I'm not Condé Nast or the guy from *Rolling Stone*, I'm just an independent guy that went out and said this is what I want to do. I had a random idea and everything just mushroomed from there.

I understand that you've been publishing *Concrete Wave* for about twelve years now. What do you think sets your magazine apart from others who are in the same space whether it's print, blog, or digital? What's your secret

to success and how you've managed to keep publishing this long?

If I go back to 1999 with *International Longboarder*, the first magazine I launched—it's actually fifteen years. But *International Longboarder* was co-owned and I only did that part-time. I've done the magazine full-time now since 2003, but your question is right, how have I kept it going for twelve years? I think two things: one, we are niche, and two, we're curiously niche, in that some of the things I've done over the years are just bizarre. I mean at one point I came up with an edition of eight different covers. You see I'm interested in people, I'm interested in the things that people do. I always felt that I wasn't publishing a magazine, I always felt like I was documenting a movement. I believe Marshall McLuhan was right when he wrote that the medium is the message, because in essence, if you want *news* about longboarding specifically, between all the blogs, the Instagrams, and the Facebooking, more is published in one day about longboarding than I could possibly publish in a lifetime.

So true.

So I've often felt that I'm not in the business of relaying information. I'm in the business of building a cult, a following, a group of people that the magazine deeply resonates with. It's almost like discovering a code or a book of codes. I don't know how to relay it to you other than that back in 1976 I was twelve years old and bought my first skateboard magazine. When I picked it up—because of the way that magazine was put together—it spoke to me as it spoke to that generation of skaters. It was like you were part of something that was so much bigger than you and there was no other way of communicating with all these skaters except through that magazine—at the time that was the only one out on the subject. Any great magazine, or any niche magazine I should say, needs to speak to your soul just as much as it speaks to your eyes and your ears.

Did you realize from the beginning that what you wanted to create or document, or be a part of, was actually a movement? Did that come later on or did you just know that from the beginning?

Yes, I knew from the very beginning. I mean, if you think about it, I would have never tumbled into this had I not been absolutely centered in my approach of, "Wow, no one else is talking about these guys, nobody else cares about them, nobody cares about these riders, it's just me." And for a long time there I had carte blanche, but now there are two other magazines on the subject and a fourth one is coming out soon so I am like the granddaddy of them all. I've become the guy that people wind up chasing, which is funny to me because I never got into it for the money, I never got into it except for one reason, I just firmly believed that the world needed to have more of this type of skateboarding—that was it!

I used to go out and teach publishing to people and would ask them, is your magazine a vitamin

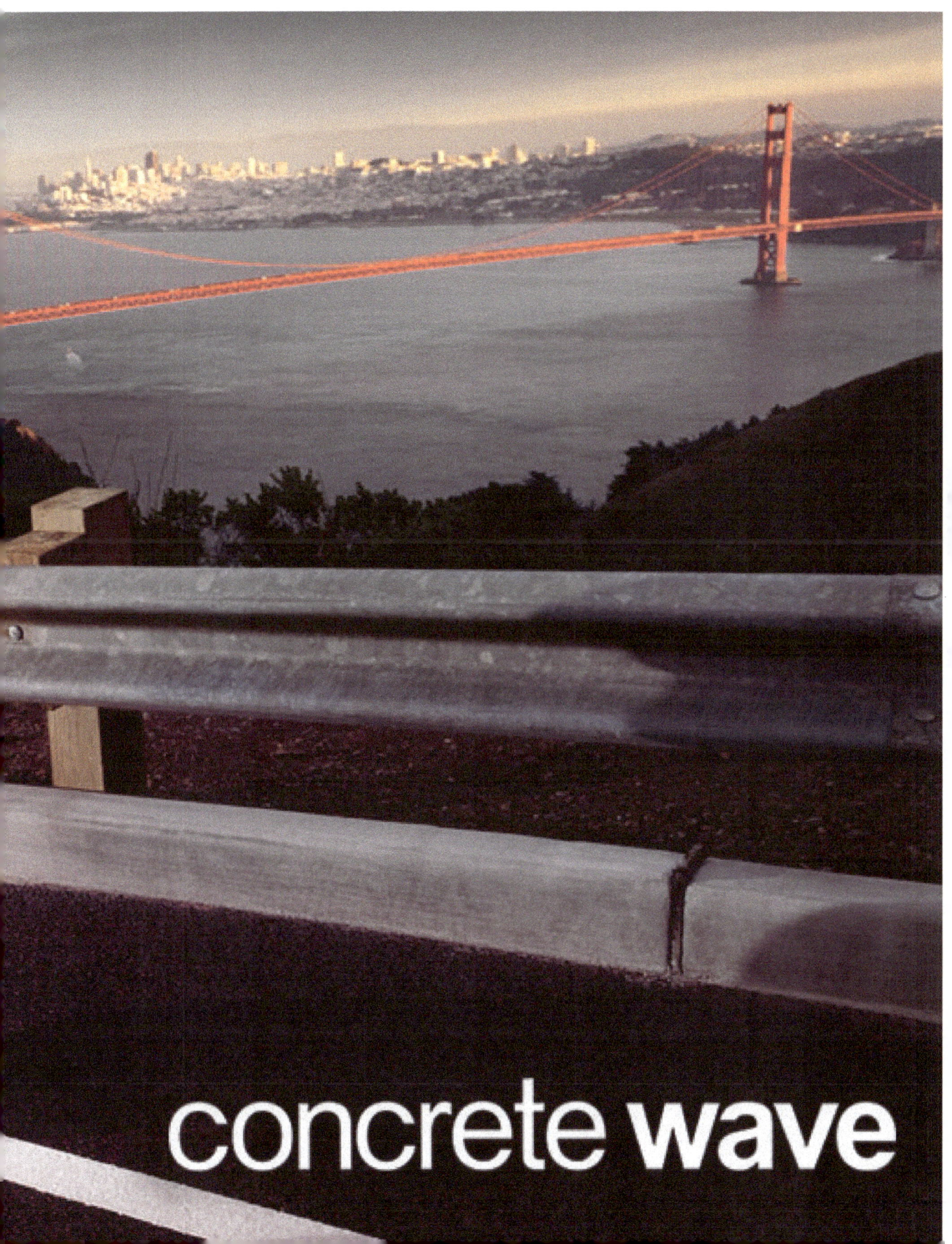

concrete wave

or is it a painkiller? And people would look at me and say, "What are you talking about?" A vitamin is good for your health and if you take it, hopefully it will restore some energy, but in the grand scheme of things it's not something that you absolutely have to have to take away something that's really burning inside of you—so a painkiller, in that sense, is more vital.

More of what I'm really talking about is this idea that people would come up to me and say, "Man, your magazine speaks to me and resonates with me." I'll have printed something four or five years ago and people come to me and say I remember that article you printed back in so and so. I mean, it's all just dead trees, right? It's just another medium, and yet I think what Marshall McLuhan said about the medium being the message, there's something about print—even with the photos I find that even the most beautiful monitors just can't do what a printed page can do. A niche magazine, when done well, just completely completes people [laughs].

So your audience must be primarily long-boarders and skateboarders?
Yes, that's pretty much it. We only make the magazine available through skateboard shops. We used to be on the newsstand but unfortunately the newsstand is not doing that great in North America at the moment.

What about the age group?
There we've actually gone down quite a bit.

We've gone from say mid-20s to lower 20s, teens, and late teens.

How are you able to keep up with the pulse of the movement as they seem to be getting younger? Is it just your love for longboarding that translates through?
I still skate but most importantly it's that I'm in constant contact with all of my advertisers, plus people send us tons of unsolicited material all the time, so I am always inundated with fresh, new information that way.

I see. How did you attract readers at the start? I understand that you were already somewhat notorious in the field.
Yes, I was known through the book but I managed to get distribution through the various skateboard brands. Well, let me back up—I always start with this idea of why. Why was I putting this magazine out there? The idea was very simple—I wanted to help change the face of skateboarding, so I felt by putting it out there for free, making it accessible, we would achieve that goal and I think we did. Still to this day I literally give 99 percent of the magazines away for free.

How do you do that? I've seen subscriptions prices, I've seen *Concrete Wave* on Issuu's digital newsstand, and I know you have apps on the various platforms, so how do you give it away for free? Is it solely funded through advertising?

Yes. You can download it for free on your iPad or your Android device, and then a few weeks later you can download it for free on Issuu, plus they're also usually available for free at skateboarding events nationwide.

The biggest component is that we never built in a model where it would be available on the newsstand. Every time it got on the newsstand we sold about 25 percent of what we'd sent, which meant that 75 percent of the magazines were being thrown away, and I figured that was not organically good.

I decided that I didn't want to play the newsstand game anymore because by the time I'd paid for everything to get out there what was coming back was an extremely negligible amount—it just wasn't making any money. For me it's cheaper to push them out there and get the shops excited, so I didn't build anything into the business model with respect to revenue from newsstand distribution.

So your advertisers get excited about the number of readers you have in your niche?
I'm not too sure. We're not audited. We've never gone after big accounts that really care about audited stuff. I often tell people, if you're going to be under 20,000 copies, chances are that most large ad agencies won't even give you the time of day.

A lot of ad agencies talk about how they love niche and how they like to engage the super-users and I've heard all kinds of stuff over the years, but ultimately I feel that ad agencies are in the business of volume and so the more money they can put out there for their clients, the more billing they will get in terms of revenue. So a $2,000 page ad—yeah, it might get some interest, but most mass market advertisers just don't care about niche, it's just way too small.

I don't like to play that game, because invariably if I got, say, Ford Motor Company putting an ad in about a new car, I don't think my audience would really care about that. It's like seeing a model railroad magazine with an ad for Tetley tea.

From what I'm understanding, you present a unique opportunity for niche advertisers within your field. It's not necessarily the big guys, but more the little, not so well-known brands, is that correct?
Absolutely. I'm all about the little guy. A lot of the time I deal with small guys who have never even dealt with the media before. Even my biggest guys still fit somewhere within the grand scheme of things. One company I worked with when I first met them were doing about five million dollars a year and now they're probably doing close to thirty million a year.

I have a little theory and my theory is called being a ball bearing or being a beach ball. As a magazine publisher I prefer to be the ball bearing which is very, very small, highly

polished, and leaves a phenomenal deep impact on you, as opposed to being a big, fluffy, colorful magazine that people see and say, "Ooh, that's a big magazine," but anything happens and it's like, "Whoa!" It gets killed by one prick.

It's very precarious doing magazines right now because a lot of people think they're publishers. "Oh, well I published this photo on Instagram, I must be a publisher," or, "I published this essay on Facebook." I tend to feel that they might be digitally publishing something but it's only because there's literally no barrier to entry, it's totally free and anybody can do it. It's like water to me but I'd rather be in the high-end vodka business, they both look the same—vodka and water look the same—but they leave completely different impressions. Plus, people tend to wash their bodies with water, they tend to brush their teeth with water, and water is used in lavatory systems. I feel like water is a great metaphor for the internet, it's like you can't live without water, but at the same time, it's not the kind of thing I want to do. I'd rather be in that little premium bond of business where people go, "Wow, this is a little niche product that has a very big impact."

You publish six times a year, how long does it take to plan and put together an issue?
Almost two months.

Can you briefly describe the process from planning the table of contents to completing in the final layout?

Yeah, it's just a mad scramble really [laughs]. It's just me weaving this whole thing together. So basically one person—me—selling the ads, getting the content, billing, collecting, doing the bookkeeping. I have an accountant now so that's a little different.

Then it's really just your personal choice, what appeals to you and what you think will appeal to your audience?
Yeah, I mean like anybody, we're going to get pressure from advertisers, we've seen that, but I also feel that in most cases we can dance that dance pretty well. Because it's skateboarding, we are extremely visual, so we lead with photos now. If the photos are what makes it work, then that's what we lead with, if the photos are marginal then we tend to run away from them.

That makes sense. So what do you find most challenging about running a magazine?
I guess the most challenging thing right now is that because of the internet people are looking at magazines very differently, but I think what's happened is that a lot of people have thrown the baby out with the bath water. I realize that it's a young person's game, I mean the kids are on their phones, reacting, interacting with friends, and I'm not suggesting getting away from that, but the biggest challenge is that although these sites get a kazillion views, what they don't have is true engagement.

I think that people have started to realize that maybe throwing print out the window wasn't the best idea because print demands attention, coupled with the fact that print is forever. But that's the challenge, trying to convince people that magazines help to build brands and help to build a whole cohesiveness around the products they sell. I can't speak for food magazines or big technology magazines because they are mass market, but what I'm talking about is niche publications.

I suppose that if you're twenty-five years old and you're put in front of a computer all day long to buy advertising or plan marketing strategies for the company that you're working for, then it seems pretty logical that you spend most of your efforts on things outside of print—after all your world is made up of digital. But I think it's a false assumption. I think you still need print, and that's my biggest task, to try to explain to people that just because you have ten thousand Facebook fans, it doesn't immediately throw print out. I strongly feel that print is something we learn right from our parent's lap, it's something we grow up with.

How does social media benefit you? What seems to work best or do you find it to be a waste of time?
I'm of two minds really. I have the Instagram followers and we're on Twitter and we have Facebook, but things happen so rapidly in terms of how many people actually get to see your posts. So part of me says, "Yeah, it's great," and our advertisers like to see that we're putting stuff out there. But in the back of my mind, I

can't help but think that all of this is just like water, it just keeps going and going and going.

Your Facebook feed is on your phone for ten seconds, you see it, you like it, and then you're on to the next thing. If anything, I think in a few years from now, someone will come up with the theory that all this just kind of devalued everything, it devalued photography, it devalued the emotions that relate to photography, and I hate to be a bummer on this, but if I look at hard, hard facts, then no, I don't think being on the internet has done a huge amount for our magazine. There are some magazines where I'm sure it's worked out really well, but in the grand scheme for me, it hasn't. I don't think I've sold more advertising as a result of it.

What do you find most rewarding about publishing a magazine? After twelve years what is it that stokes your fire?
You know, I used to say that the worst day in publishing a skateboard magazine is better than the best day selling photocopiers—and you can quote me on that. I'm actually going through a pretty interesting time, so if you ask me what keeps me going or what makes this work, I'll answer by telling you that when I see people who have never experienced this before—as I said, I actually go out and teach this stuff.

Two and a half years ago I built something called Longboarding for Peace, which is basically another movement, only there's literally nothing financial about the movement. It's just a movement of peace, balance, and justice. I go around the world doing it. I started in Israel in the Palestine territories and I had Arabs and Israelis skateboard with each other. Then I go to First Nations kids and then I go to kids in Houston. I have all these people doing all this stuff. I mean, we have people giving blood and we have shoe drives and we work with the police on gun buy-back programs, where we take guns off the streets and trade them in for longboards. I do all these crazy things because I realize that when people get the chance to experience the freedom of a skateboard, it can really be used to propel them.

I always thought that my tombstone would read, "He helped change the face of skateboarding," but I realize now that it has to be changed to, "He helped change the face of the world."

Wow!
And if you really want to know what keeps me going it's that I keep my eye on the prize. I put things in motion that may take me thirty years, but there's enough stuff happening that my little magazine was a catalyst for, and I guess what I'll leave you with is this. If you go back to the original definition of what a magazine is, it's got nothing to do with print. It's an Arabic word, and a magazine was a room or place for storing gunpowder or explosives and it's one of those things where, if you think about it, it's a really good definition of something that really affects us—it sort of blows our minds.

The truth is that I believe I'm delivering some pretty explosive information, and if the original meaning of a magazine has to do with ammunition, then I would say that's pretty cool. So if you think of it from that perspective, that what you're dealing with is very powerful information, a very powerful medium, I think that propels you through. It gives you a sense of, "Yeah, this is hitting people in a very unique way," and it can lead to some other amazing things, and that's the power of a magazine. It gives you a perspective as a publisher to really be the poster child, if you will, the symbol for the movement that is behind your magazine.

My final question was going to be what last message of wisdom or inspiration would you have for someone who may be considering launching their own publication, but to me, you just gave the answer.
I guess so, but that's what I was saying, don't publish a magazine—document a movement. That's all you really can do now because of the internet—as much as you want to write about chocolate covered ants, there's already a website about it out there. As much as you want to publish a magazine on left-handed guitar players, there's already a website out there about it. So the question is, "How do you harness the energy of a particular tribe that you want to really immerse yourself with?"

I can really appreciate everything you're saying. I'm about to join the movement myself, that's how bad it is [laughs].

Well, if you can appreciate it, that's what I've dedicated my life to. I'll leave you with one final piece of the puzzle.

Okay.
It was never about the magazine.

I can see that.
It was about an instrument or something that would trigger conversations, that would get people excited, and would start something else happening. I've had dozens of people get jobs because of this magazine. I've had dozens of companies stay the course because there was a write-up about them in the magazine. I've had dozens of people tell me, "Your magazine was that catalyst," and they've said it in many different ways—ultimately that's a pretty amazing position to be in. That's how I feel. It's always about the people and a magazine publisher should always go back to people.

Michael, I'm not going to ask you for another thing, that was brilliant.
Lorraine, I want to thank you and I'm going to have you look over my Longboarding for Peace website. The address is longboardingforpeace. org. I hope you've had fun with this, I most certainly have.

I sure did, and I get it—it's all about the message, and we use different formats but ultimately it's the same message and that's why I'm doing this now. So when I say I get it, I truly do. Thanks so much.

My pleasure. Things always have a way of working out!

The Slow Journalism magazine
A new perspective on
the events that mattered

Delayed Gratification

Delayed Gratification

Delayed Gratification

Delayed Gratification

Delayed Gratification

DELAYED GRATIFICATION

ROB ORCHARD

Magazine name: *Delayed Gratification*
Director: Rob Orchard
Year founded: 2011
Tagline: Last to breaking news
Editorial mission: To provide an antidote to super-speedy digital news production with a slow, considered approach that returns to stories after the dust has settled
Location: London, UK
Website: slow-journalism.com
Formats: Print and blog
Issues per year: Four
Language: English
Reach: Worldwide
Available: Website and independent bookstores
Circulation: 5,000+
Price per issue: £10 (approx. $15 USD)
One-year subscription: £35 (approx. $53 USD)
Size of in-house team: Four full-time

Lorraine: Rob, what was you up to before you decided to launch your magazine?
Rob: Before I launched the magazine I had a customer publishing company in Dubai where we published magazines for big companies like Virgin Atlantic. I did that for about three and a half years before starting the Slow Journalism Company.

What made you decide to do your own thing?
I was about to turn thirty and didn't want to do customer magazines any more as they can be immensely frustrating. If you get great clients like Virgin, then you have the opportunity to do some great work, which can be extremely rewarding. On the other hand, if you get clients who don't really understand what you're doing and apply a lot of restrictions, it can turn out to be very frustrating because naturally as journalists all we want to do is uncover a good story and tell the truth. But with customer publishing all you're really doing is making slightly fancier leaflets and marketing collateral for companies, and I just got to a stage where I realized that if I didn't do something else now, I was going to end up doing that for another ten years or so, when what I really wanted to do was launch a magazine I could be proud of.

Did you do any market research prior to launching your magazine?
No we didn't. In retrospect that was a very stupid thing, because of course, successful businesses generally identify a need first and then figure out how to cater to that need. We just wanted to create a magazine that we wanted to read and then see if an audience would coalesce around it from there—which makes for a really good magazine but not necessarily a brilliant business. There were five of us that launched this together and all of us were either journalists or editors. We didn't have a single marketing expert, subscriptions expert, or advertising sales expert—none of us even had

basic accounting skills. So what we had was the potential for a really great magazine, but not necessarily a super smart business.

How did you select your magazine's title?

We took a lot of time over it and there was a lot of back and forth between us. We wanted something that was striking, intelligent, and would capture what it was that we were trying to do. We thought of calling it *The Slow Journal* and *The Slow News*. We had all sorts of weird names but luckily we didn't go for any of those. In the end the group was basically split: two really disliked *Delayed Gratification* while the rest of us thought it was great. It's almost like naming a child—you go through agony trying to think of a name for it but, as with all these things, once you actually launch it and see it, whatever it is settles into its name and it turns out to be just fine.

How did you initially fund your magazine?

My main business partner, Marcus, and I put in about two or three thousand pounds apiece. Not a huge amount but just enough to get us going at the beginning. Then we sold three or four hundred subscriptions to our family and friends before we launched, which gave us enough money for our initial print run. As we were journalists ourselves, we knew lots of other journalists in the field so we were able to call in a couple of favors. It was really hand-to-mouth for a very long time there but the main thing was selling those subscriptions and getting that money up front.

What was your initial print run?

Twelve hundred copies.

What was the original concept behind the magazine? I know slow journalism, but how did you actually define that?

The magazine was set up to champion two things. The first thing was print, because when we were putting the magazine together loads of people were talking about the death of print as a lot of the big titles were going out of business. We thought the whole thing was nonsense, we felt that people would continue to want print, but that if you were going to do a print magazine then you had to do the very best that print could be. So make it beautiful with high production values, beautiful paper stock, take care with the whole tactile experience and all the other lovely things that you get from a really well made print product.

The second thing we set out to champion was perspective. When we were launching—and ever since then, actually—we've seen the speed of news production and distribution increase tremendously while at the same time there's been a massive disinvestment in media in general. There's been the slashing of editorial budgets and staff across the board, so what you had was fewer people with fewer resources being asked to do more work, faster and faster. Inevitably that leads to errors and strange practices, with the use of PR and all sorts of devices just to fill up the space. What we wanted to do was say, "Look, we don't want to join everybody else in trying to be the first in news. That's not our interest and that's not where we're at. But what we are interested in is being at the other end of it—so once everybody else has stopped talking about the stories, three months down the line or so, we want to revisit them with the benefit of hindsight and see what's really changed and what we can add in terms of analysis, overview, and context."

Also, I think there's a function in terms of curating. Every single day two or three hundred news stories come at you and a lot of them are just fluff and nonsense, but with so much happening all at once it can be difficult to tell what's what. Our idea was to look back after three months and get rid of all the nonsense, get rid of all the Twitter fights, all the PR nonsense that gets into the news, all the bogus surveys, the celebrity crap, and all that sort of thing, and return to what was *really* important at the time.

So who is the magazine aimed at? What does your audience look like?
When we launched the magazine we really had no idea who our audience would be. I think there are three types of magazines. There's the magazine that carefully works out the demographic that it wants to hit and then builds the magazine around that. Then there's another type of magazine that works out what type of advertising it wants and then builds the magazine around that. We're the third type of magazine, where you make something that

you'd like to read yourself and hope that people are going to be drawn to it—and so for a long time we never knew much about our readers.

Last year, however, we conducted our first readership survey and discovered that there were two distinct clumps. There were people in their twenties and thirties who tended to be design driven who enjoyed the infographics, then there were people in their fifties and sixties who wanted this slower approach to news.

We also get another perspective on our audience when we see the gift messages that come through. We get a lot of parents buying the magazine for their kids as they go off to university saying things like, "You don't read newspapers but maybe you'll read this." Then we get a lot people buying the magazine as retirement gifts with the thinking that as the retiree will have more time on their hands, maybe it will be something they'd enjoy reading. Obviously there's a broad mix in general, but there are a few distinct pockets and I think people like different things. I think a lot of people just buy us for the infographics and a lot buy us for the longform features.

What can you tell me about distribution? Did you have distribution for your first issue?
No we didn't, we always saw it being primarily driven by subscriptions from the website, as we thought that it would sit quite strangely on the newsstand next to all of these other weekly and monthly titles. To have a quarterly title

An actor

STATE AND MAIN
ALMOST FAMOUS

PUNCH-DRUNK LOVE

LOVE LIZA

MY BOYFRIEND'S BACK
MONEY FOR NOTHING
JOEY BREAKER
MR. JEALOUSY
LEAP OF FAITH
NEXT STOP, WONDERLAND
SCENT OF A WOMAN

NOBODY'S FOOL
THE GETAWAY
WHEN A WOMAN...

MAGNOLIA
FLAWLESS
THE BIG LEBOWSKI
PATCH ADAMS
HAPPINESS

*95%

$864,600,000

Tor

rver of the late
an

Christian Tate

Delayed
Gratification

The Slow Journalism magazine
A new perspective on
the events that
mattered

£15

that actually looks back on news, we felt that it was going to be a job to try to sell people into it. Luckily, that's changed since then and we've now got quite good distribution in London. We have good international distribution as well, which in some aspects is even better than what we have here in the UK. For example, we're in three stores in Jakarta, Indonesia, but not in any here in Birmingham, which is absolutely insane to me.

The real problem for independent magazines is this issue of distribution costs, because the whole architecture of magazine distribution is built around the old style of publishing, around big magazines that sell hundreds of thousands of copies at a very low rate because they're primarily funded by advertising. With that model, you could get away with a lot of magazines coming back unsold and if the cover price covered your shipping costs that was fine, but obviously with independent magazines that's not the case because we're printing small numbers and as a result it costs us much more per issue to print.

Generally with independent magazines each individual magazine is not a disposable object, it has to be perfect bound, has to be a decent size, and it just kills us when people rip off the covers and send them back because they've been unable to sell them. Independent magazines just don't have the infrastructure that they need in place. Although we do have newsstand sales, we see it almost as a necessary marketing exercise more than anything else because it's very difficult to make any money back that way.

Okay. As far as marketing and publicizing the magazine, has social media been good to you? Yes, definitely. But for a very long time we swore off social media partly because the magazine is set up to counter social-media-driven news and so for a long time we just didn't know what to do with it. If you look at our Facebook page you'll see that we launched in 2011 and then there was nothing for two years, just empty space and the sound of tumbleweeds. But luckily for us we got a fantastic assistant editor who's a bit younger than us and understands that kind of stuff and has developed a blog that automatically feeds into our social media accounts. She's been with us for about a year and has already doubled or tripled our number of Twitter followers and the number of likes on our Facebook page.

Right now we're tentatively looking at doing some marketing over social media channels as well. We do still have this slightly ambivalent feeling towards it because, like most people, I think that most of the stuff on there is just space-filling nonsense. I think it's such a strange thing to think that after we die, all of our witless, nonsense thoughts, and tweets are going to be sitting on a server somewhere and I don't feel great about adding to that. But I think we've found a format that works, so instead of having to give content away for free online, we got smart about it and found interesting, useful things to write about that were around the stories we covered. Like behind the scenes stories, or we'll do an interview with someone who's written something for us, and things along those lines, rather than just giving away our features for free.

So that's basically your social media strategy as far as handling that animal?
Yes, exactly.

As a quarterly magazine, does it typically take about three months to put an issue together?
Yeah. It's kind of an ongoing constant process of commissioning, editing, and moving stuff through. As with all magazines, it definitely builds to a crescendo towards the end where there are sixteen-hour days and working throughout the night. But yes, it's a constant process that takes place over three months.

I'm not saying that the process would be any easier, but I should imagine that at least you don't have the added pressure of time as far delivering the news stories. Is that correct?
Yes, that's absolutely fair. We try to make the most out of that, so we'll send journalists off on stories for months at a time. We try to do a design that will last for three months and give readers lots of content to look at over the three-month period. We try our best to benefit from having a lovely, long production cycle.

What do you find to be the most challenging part of running a magazine?

The economics, because it's not an easy way to make money. In fact, almost everything is geared towards you not making any money out of it, particularly if you're a print-first publication. It is challenging but a challenge can be good as well, you just need to be smarter about it and think harder about it, but that is definitely the most difficult thing.

What's most rewarding about publishing *Delayed Gratification*?
Ideas. Just having those editorial meetings particularly at the beginning of the cycle where you're just thinking about how you can make the next issue absolutely amazing and thinking of all these brilliant new sections, new ideas, new features that you can commission—amazing artwork and things like that I absolutely love. That's the best thing in the world to me.

What factors do you think contribute to the success of a magazine in general?
I think a magazine really needs to be very clear on what it's for. I think there are a huge number of magazines that are just vanity projects. Food, travel, and fashion tend to be things that people are really interested in, but unless they're bringing something new to the table I think they're probably doomed because of all the noise that's out there.

There are so many new launches all the time and people's attention spans are understandably minute because we're all bombarded with

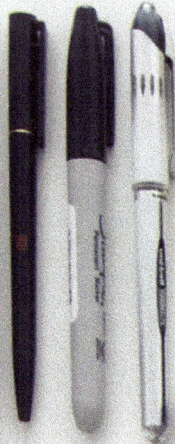

Welcome to
**Delayed
Gratification**

This is the first issue of your subscription to
DG, the Slow Journalism magazine.

If you move house please contact us at
subs@dgquarterly.com/0207 209 1008
and let us know your new address.

If you would like to introduce a friend to the
magazine, please pass on the promo code
'slowtuesday', which will give them a
10 percent discount on subscriptions bought
through www.dgquarterly.com.

We hope you enjoy the magazine.

All the best,
Marcus and Rob
Directors, The Slow Journalism Company

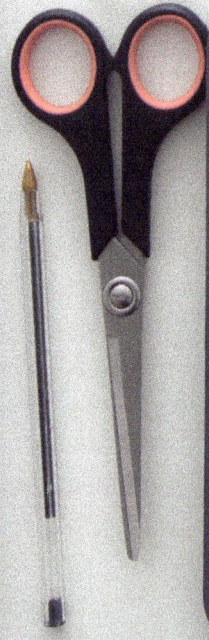

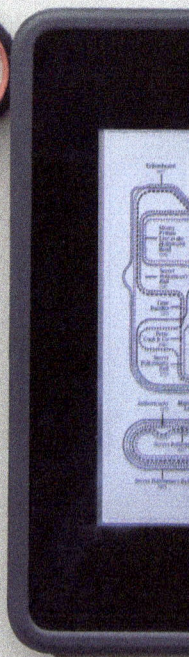

STAEDTLER
Textsurfer classic

SONY

REC/PAUSE   PLAY/STOP

ENTER

Del
Grafation

Delayed
Gratification

The Slow Journalism magazine
A new perspective on
the events that
mattered

£12

**THE WORLD'S
FIRST SLOW
JOURNALISM
MAGAZINE**

LOOKING BACK AT
THE BIG EVENTS OF
SUMMER 2013

**INSIDE
THIS ISSUE**

When Anonymous
took on Los Zetas

The engineer from
Derby who became
a king in Nigeria

Everything that
ever happened to
Alan Partridge

The brave new world
of glow-in-the-dark
cats and balding mice •
Soccer and sabre-rattling in
Gibraltar • Inside Nairobi's
Westgate Mall siege • The
difficult birth of Battersea
Power Station • Confessions
of a whistleblower •

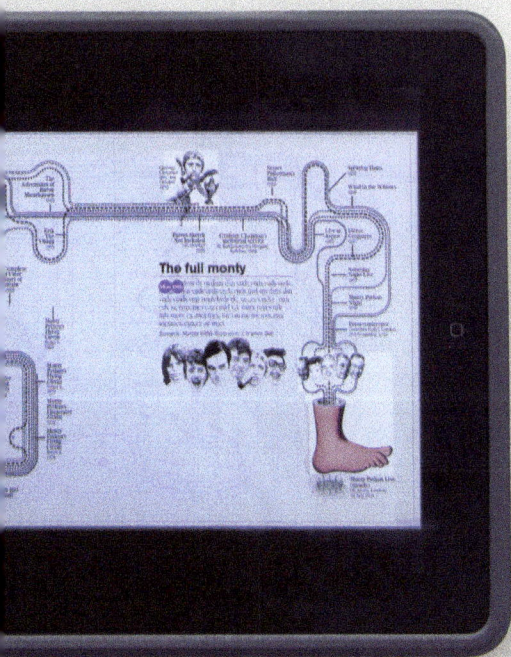

so many different options on a daily basis. You could be watching Netflix, or listening to a podcast, or downloading *The Times* on your phone, or reading a million blogs. So actually standing out in the middle of all that and getting a slice of people's limited attention spans is incredibly difficult, that's why I think the number one thing is that the magazine needs to know what it's for. It needs to be good looking, there's no sense in making a magazine if it's not beautifully designed. It needs to have sensational content, which means brilliant writers who have written really well and have been tightly edited. The magazine needs to develop a relationship with its reader. It's quite difficult for independent magazines when a lot of them are just quarterly or even biannual because you're not getting into people's lives super often, but I think holding regular events can help with that.

Events? You mean holding them throughout the year so a magazine can stay in the front of people's minds?
Yes, exactly.

What about its failure? What do you think can contribute to a magazine's failure?
I think the number one thing for success is the Woody Allen thing of just turning up, because a huge number of magazines die off on issue three or four and it's because the money's not there. The initial enthusiasm has been lost plus it's not really found its readership. I think the ones that do survive survive because they

doggedly keep pushing on. It was very tough for us in our second year. There were a lot of times where we thought, "Should we pack it all in? Is this kind of daft?" But each time what kept us going was just how excited we were about producing the next issue, and so eventually we got through. You can have the best marketing in the world, the best PR and all that type of thing, but you need to keep slogging away and building up those numbers and trying to stop the bucket from leaking too much at the bottom.

Are you currently profitable?
Yes, definitely. We broke even at the beginning of last year. So now we run at a profit, we're able to pay people properly. I wouldn't say that we're doing outrageously well. We've never had adverts in the magazine, so we've never had that as a revenue stream—all profits arise through sales and subscriptions.

Where would you say most of those sales come from? Is it online or individual stores?
70 percent of it is through our online shop and our online subscriptions.

So how are people finding you?
We do quite a lot of PR. We do a lot of events and features. We also get interviewed a lot, which is nice. We do inserts in other magazines. We do insert swaps and also do them with subscription services. We're starting to look at possibly targeting people through Facebook and Google advertising as well. I'm

also looking into podcast advertising. Right now the vast majority of people are finding out about us through word of mouth and our efforts to talk our current readers and subscribers into introducing the magazine to their friends or giving them gift subscriptions.

Do you currently send out a weekly or monthly newsletter?

Yes, we do. It's been semi-regular for the last year, but next year we plan to send it out weekly and it's going to feature the best content from the blog and the occasional longform feature from the archives.

So the no-ad strategy—is that something you plan to stick with?

Yes it is, because what we always wanted to do was to show that you could make an editorial business work just by getting people to pay for content. The magazine is never going to be a mass-market thing, it just isn't, but we'll always fight to keep the numbers up. Doing it this way means that you charge a proper amount—it's thirty six pounds a year or ten pounds a copy—but it also means that we don't have to get involved with that whole horrible, murky world of advertising. We don't have to find and pitch people and chase after their money, we don't have to do any of that.

I'd be a fool to completely rule it out forever, because if somebody came to me tomorrow and said I'll take twenty pages for this advertiser whose products I love and he ethically

agrees to pay a hundred thousand pounds, I'd say, "Yes please." But we're quite proud of the fact that we've managed to make this work without having to scout for ads.

It's quite an amazing business model actually. What types of skills or disciplines do you think are important for a publisher to have today?

That's a really good question. This isn't really a skill or a discipline, but if you're going to do an independent magazine you have to really, really love what you do because otherwise you're not going to make it through the task of trying to pull the whole thing together and keep it going. You've got to live and breathe it. You've got to love it, otherwise you're not going to have the will to carry it on.

I think it can really help if you're willing and able to do some promotion if you feel comfortable talking. We generate a lot of our interest by either one of my partners or me talking at events, being articulate and interesting—I think that's really good.

You also need to be able to spot opportunities—we do quite a lot of infographics teaching and that helps with the money, as well as with the magazine. Being a good editor or employing a good editor is important because with an independent magazine quite often you don't offer a gigantic amount of money to the people who write for you, but if you can offer some really intelligent editing, writers respond well

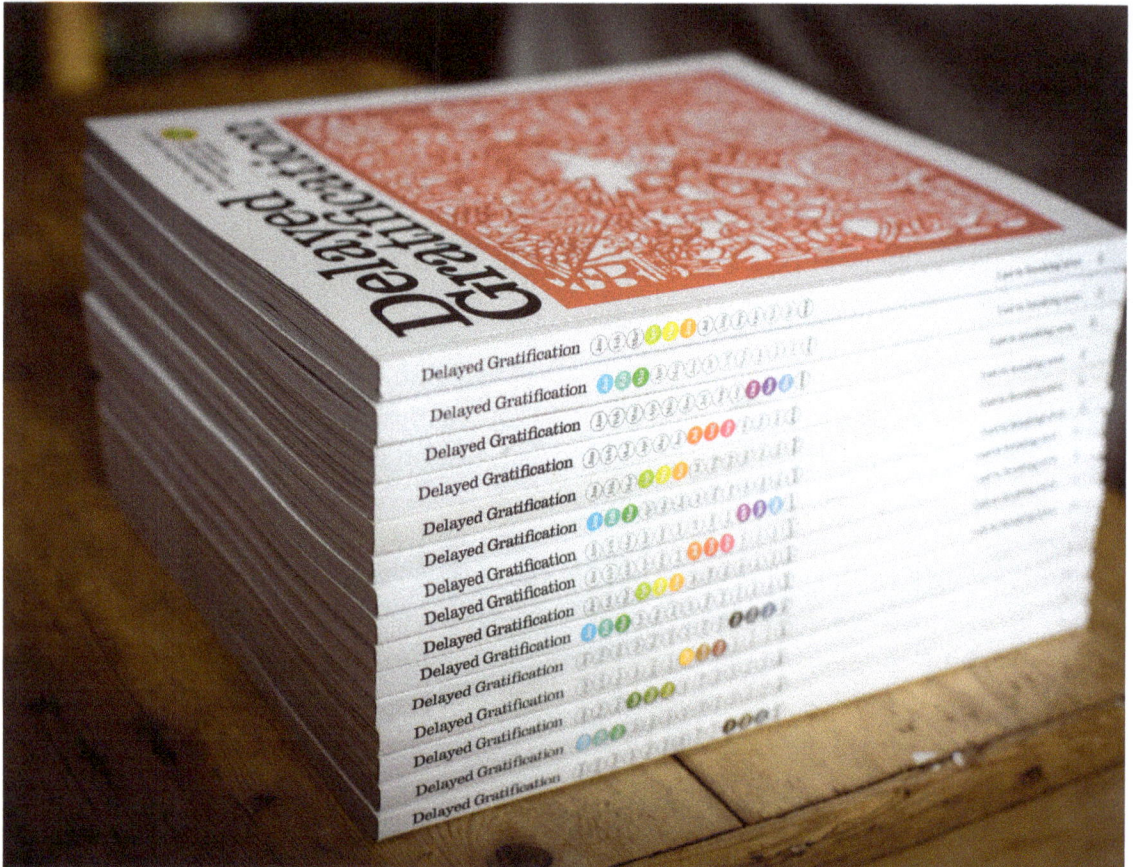

to that. Whenever I do freelance work part of me is happy when they say, "Oh yeah, fine, I'll just go through it myself," but what I really want is somebody who will say, "Yeah, I like this but we can make it 20 percent better if you change this, this, and this." So I think being (or having) a good editor is great.

Another skill which I don't have, unfortunately, is being really, really smart about the money, being good with budgets and accounts, and being on top of it all, because as a small business most times, initially at least, it will

have major cash flow issues and you need to be able to keep all the various plates spinning at the same time. Those are probably the most useful skills.

You mentioned something that stuck with me. I was going to ask, what do you do in addition to the magazine that contributes to the bottom line?

Yes, we do teaching. We teach feature writing and infographics design at the *Guardian*. We've done the occasional piece of corporate work that helps bring in money for the magazine, things like creating infographics for them and doing magazine-type things for companies.

So basically you share your expertise with different companies?
Yes, exactly.

Finally, what last message or insight do you have for a reader who may be thinking about launching a magazine?
[Laughs] I would say don't do it. Don't do it unless you're so totally driven to do it that you know and are prepared not to be properly paid for a good couple of years, maybe even three years—you really need to make sure that you're happy to do that. You have to be happy to lavish all your time and attention on this thing because it's going to need a lot of attention to make it grow and make it work.

I would say don't do it unless you've got a really brilliant, unique idea that is going to resonate with people. Certainly don't do it if it's just going to be like another travel magazine, another food magazine, or another whatever. The market doesn't need them, it's already overrun and it's going to be very difficult to get people inspired and excited by it unless it's something brilliantly new.

Don't do it unless you've got people to do it with, because it can be terribly lonely if you don't have a nice team of people that you get along with well and you've worked out some of the ideas with in advance. So basically don't

do it unless you've got those three things in place, and if you have them then definitely do it because it's the most fun way you can spend your time. Making magazines is incredibly fun and if you can actually make money from it then it's even better!

Disegno.

No.6

DESIGN
ARCHITECTURE
FASHION
BIANNUAL
S/S 2014

UK £8
US $19

Nathalie Du Pasquier

Konstantin Grcic constructs the future. The new Medici. Remembering Lina Bo Bardi.
The importance of colour. Boudicca reshapes couture. An essay on forests and design.
Azzedine Alaïa on the legacy of Charles James.

DISEGNO

JOHANNA
AGERMAN ROSS

Magazine name: *Disegno*
Founder and editor in chief: Johanna Agerman Ross
Year founded: 2011
Tagline: The culture of design
Editorial mission: *Disegno* is the leading biannual magazine dedicated to international architecture, design, and fashion
Location: London, UK
Website: disegnodaily.com
Formats: Print, blog, and events
Issues per year: Two
Language: English
Reach: Worldwide
Available: Website, digital newsstands, select newsstands, and bookstores
Circulation: 35,000
Price per issue: £8.00 ($19 USD)
One-year subscription: £28.00 (approx. $42 USD)
Size of in-house team: Three full-time and three part-time

Lorraine: Johanna, what was you up to before you started your magazine?
Johanna: I worked as an editor for *Icon* magazine and actually left to start the research for *Disegno*. I have a background in fashion journalism and design history. I earned a BA in fashion promotion at the London College of Fashion and then did my masters at the Royal College of Art in design history. I have had journalism, design, and fashion interests from a long time back.

Would you say that's from childhood?
Yes, I think so. Although retired now, both my parents worked within the creative industry. My mother was an architect and my father a curator and director of a design museum. So yes, design and architecture have always been a part of my life in one form or another.

After you left *Icon*, what was your initial thinking with regards to *Disegno*?

I left *Icon* at the end of December, 2010, so from January of 2011 onwards I worked on figuring out what the magazine would contain and exactly what it would be. Would it be online? Would it be a printed object? Or would it consist of a series of events? I quickly came to the conclusion that I wanted it to be all three: to have a web presence, be a printed object, as well as hold events like talks and seminars in a way that would allow me to bring the topic of design to a much wider audience and make it accessible to more people.

At the time I didn't see any other magazine business models that included all three aspects from the very beginning (as within this industry things usually happen bit by bit) but I wanted to launch all three aspects together. So after completing the research I worked on building up the content and then creating the identity. We launched the website in September and launched the first issue a month or so later. We

also did an event at the same time. So overall, I guess I had a nine-month research period.

As far as the research goes, what exactly were you checking into?
A lot of my research was more about creating awareness. I went to all the big events surrounding design, architecture, and fashion. I made sure I went to a lot of places. I was in Milan for the Milan furniture fair, for example (which is the biggest design fair in the whole world) to talk about the magazine and let people know that I had this plan and to make sure that they were both interested in it and could see the point of it.

So you gauged interest?
Yes, just to make sure that people felt there was a need for it. I quickly established that there was, as people felt that in-depth reporting and longform journalism—which the printed version of *Disegno* now contains—wasn't really present in many other places at the time, although the market has changed a little since.

I knew the website would offer something a little less unique because it was more about having continuous contact with our readers. As we come out just twice a year, it's important for people not to forget about us in between, so the website presented a way for us to publish the stories that had our flavor and tone, and had been researched by us but were not necessarily as long as the articles that are found within the magazine.

Overall I felt that a lot of the online design and fashion journalists were quite un-journalistic, often relying on a press release rather than their own research, and I wanted to apply the same rules to *Disegno* online as I did to the magazine. I think that sometimes people see fashion and design as something that doesn't have to be treated in the same way as subjects like finance or politics, but I feel it's very important to approach it in a serious manner in terms of how you write and report on it.

So you're saying that you have strict editorial rules for your online content?
Yes, exactly—definitely.

Did you initially develop a business plan or was it somewhat of a rough outline?
Yes, I had a business plan, although it was not in depth as far as the financial aspect was concerned. I knew where I wanted the revenue to come from but it was very difficult that early on to know or guesstimate what we could expect to generate from magazine or advertising sales, whether from print or online. So it was an outline that basically said, "Okay, we have a magazine that's printed twice a year, we have the website, and we have an events program, this is how I see this developing and how the different strands can support each other."

I do think that business plans are important and I would say, for me, it was more important to do a proper business plan later on, as about a year after I started I had a much better idea about the business and could really gauge what to expect from the different elements.

That is probably somewhat unconventional, because normally you would set up a plan from the start. But I knew from the beginning that there would be no money coming in from the business—at least in the first year—and therefore it would basically have to be supported by my own savings and the income I could generate from other places.

Is that how you initially funded the magazine?
Yes. I saved a lot of money while I was working so that I could support myself, but I also made sure to take a lot of jobs that were well paid but didn't take up all my time. So, for example, consulting or copy writing for brands—things I found fairly easy to do but didn't require a lot of my time. I made sure I had enough, not only to support myself, but also to be able to put away a little bit to publish the magazine.

As you know, your most expensive cost is paper and printing, so I tried to get those sponsored for the first issue. Writers for the website and magazine were not paid at the beginning, but I think that in this day and age when you start something independently, that is fairly common practice. It's not something people frown upon if they feel you have a good idea and that you're doing it for all the right reasons.

How did the name *Disegno* come about?
Well, it's Italian and it comes from when I was studying the history of design at the Royal College of Art. We had a whole course called Design Versus Disegno at the Victoria and Albert Museum. Nowadays, disegno means sketch or design, but in the sixteenth or seventeenth century—during the Italian Renaissance—disegno had more to do with being able to communicate creative ideas on paper. So having a vision for something, putting that creative idea on paper, and then eventually realizing it as a real object. I liked the connotations, that it meant more than one thing as well as the fact that the word "design" is actually derived from it—so that's where the name came from.

You say the name is Italian, are you Italian?
No, I am Swedish [laughs].

Who would you say is your primary audience?
Initially I thought that the readership would be a broad design-interested audience. But then I quickly understood that people who are interested in design and architecture often work within that sector, so if the magazine is to talk about things in a really in-depth way it is going to be the people who work professionally within those fields who are going to be the most interested in it. Based on that I would say that the audience consists of architects, designers, and people that write about those particular subjects. Not so much fashion at the moment because as a title we are not very well known within the fashion industry, but it is something that we're working on.

[1] Antonello da Messina (c.1430-1479) was a Sicilian-born Renaissance painter strongly influenced by early Netherlandish paintings.

[2] Interbau was a large-scale architecture project in West Berlin in 1957 that took the form of a exhibition. Only part of the development was completed in time; the remaining 35 buildings were added by 1960.

[3] Stalinallee (now Karl-Marx-Allee) was a monumental boulevard in East Berlin built by the GDR in the 1950s. Its socialist-style towers were designed by Egon Hartmann, Hanns Hopp, Kurt W. Leucht, Richard Paulick and Karl Souradny, bookended with towers by Hermann Henselmann (1905-1995) in the wedding-cake style of socialist classicism.

n room 62 of the National Gallery in London hangs a small painting by 15th-century Sicilian artist Antonello da Messina.[1] Little bigger than an A3 sheet of paper, it portrays 4th-century Christian theologian Saint Jerome reading in his study – a peculiar piece of miniature architecture, or a very large piece of furniture, sitting within a vast ecclesiastical space. At its base, small steps lead up to a platform where Jerome sits in deep concentration. The shelves behind him contain various objects of symbolic and religious nature, while arched windows reveal a view of a field, a town and birds in flight. "That picture has been important to me for a long time," says German industrial designer Konstantin Grcic. "It's in my library of references."

A three-room apartment in an Alvar Aalto-designed building in Hansaviertel, Berlin, is Grcic's equivalent of Jerome's study – a quiet retreat from his Munich studio. He has a view of the other buildings in the Interbau[2] estate, which was initiated on the occasion of 1957's International Building Exhibition. It was West Berlin's response to Hermann Henselmann et al.'s no-less-famous East Berlin socialist building project Stalinallee,[3] created during the Cold War when buildings functioned as propaganda for political systems on either side of the Wall. In the west, celebrated international architects such as Arne Jacobsen and Oscar Niemeyer were commissioned to rebuild Hansaviertel adjacent to Berlin's central park, the Tiergarten. Today, the area is quiet and green, and many residents remain from its inauguration more than 50 years ago. The well-preserved buildings make it a much-visited design destination, but compared to the bustling central neighbourhoods that have come to define Berlin in recent years, it's something of an oddity.

Grcic retreats to Berlin for about 10 days a month. The rest of the time, if he's not travelling, he spends in Munich. "The Berlin space has an element of freedom to it," says Grcic, wearing what seems to have become a uniform: dark-rimmed glasses, dark jeans, a navy sweater, a dark-blue blazer and his hair slicked-back. His high-top black leather loafers are pristine; he looks comfortable, but smart. "I am so used to working with assistants and having constant dialogue and distraction, so being on my own is a very strong experience," he says. "I'm confronted with my own limitations, which is nice as it forces me to think twice and a little harder."

Such reflection is typical of Grcic. Even 25 years into a successful career as an industrial designer, he remains restless and humble. He has weathered 1990s minimalism, the ostentation of the 2000s and the recent recession, and given into none. Instead, he has cultivated his own language, creating objects and furniture that push boundaries of both manufacture and use. Chairs by Grcic such as 360° and Chair One for Italian furniture manufacturer Magis became instantly recognisable expressions of the early 21st-century and its modes of production. His largest forthcoming project however – developed over three years – is not a product or piece of furniture. It is an exhibition, a format to which Grcic feels close. "Exhibition-making feels very familiar to me," he says. "My mother had an art gallery and exhibitions were a part of the

A tubular steel chair from
from the Midtown project
for Muji sits under the Pipe
desk for Muji-Thonet in one
room of the apartment.
In the foreground is
Grcic's School side-table,
manufactured by Böwer.

Starting out, how did you attract readers? I know you said that you attended many different events.

Yes, that was a really big part as I collected business cards and built up a database of people I could contact once the website and magazine were launched.

Did you have a huge email list?

No, although it has grown quite a lot since then. I guess as I worked in the industry for so many years before, it wasn't like I had to start from scratch. I already had a lot of contacts, which I think was really great. Initially, a lot of my promotion consisted of word of mouth where I would speak to people about the magazine, they would think it was a great idea and in turn tell others. We also had Comag as a distributor from the beginning and they were very good in terms of securing placement in stores that have readership that's interested in these types of magazines.

How did you go about getting distribution right at the beginning before they had even seen a printed copy of the magazine?

That's a good question, because I guess it takes a certain belief on their side in your product; but because I had already worked within the industry before and had some contacts, I was able to call the people I already knew and say, "I'm doing my own thing now and it's going to look like this." I was able to draw on what I had already done to explain to them what the new product would be.

It's not a big loss for a distributor when they take the magazine on as a free product and then only pay me if they sell it. Of course, it needs to be of a certain standard and quality, and have a defined look and so forth, but I was able to show pages of what I expected it to look like. Also the art director, Daren Ellis, is fairly well known within the industry so it was advantageous that we had a good name attached to the magazine.

How did you go about finding and reaching new readers and subscribers at the time?

Social media was important for that, although we are now at a stage where we need to build it up more. We are three years old and I feel that we have kind of puttered a bit in terms of the people who are visiting our website and also the people who pick up the magazine; so earlier this year I took a distributor agent on board who is working with us to place the magazine in new stores internationally. Through them we've managed to secure a place in Barnes & Noble in the States. So expanding distribution is definitely a great way of growing readership.

More often than not, whatever actions you take will require money, so I decided to invest in working with an agent who does worldwide distribution. When a magazine has a big publishing house behind it, it can do loads of advertising, taking billboard ads, etc., but that's not available to an independent publisher like me, so it's really just making sure that the magazine gets out there as much as possible. For the website we actually just launched a redesign today. We've made it much easier to navigate, which should result in people staying on the site longer. That provides another way for us to grow readership in a roundabout sort of way.

Did you hire a professional design company or is that something you do in-house?

Yeah, that's something we did in-house. We have an art director and a creative director. I worked with our creative director on the changes. It doesn't look significantly different as there are just a few additions to it. And then in terms of the functions, we work with our web developer who is a freelancer and is actually the person I've worked with since the first launch. I've been rather lucky with *Disegno*, as ever since we launched three years ago I am still working with all of the same people.

Really?

Yes. The same printer, the same paper company, the same designers, the same writers, the same subeditor—apart from one of them who got a full-time job elsewhere. But I've been very lucky to be able to work, and continue working, with the same people as it just means that it's easier to collaborate and move forward. I mean we are growing—like in this room there are many more people now than in the beginning, but the people who were with us from the start are still here.

That says a lot. How many people do you have working in-house?

Well, for the magazine there's me, Oli Stratford the deputy editor, and Anya Lawrence our editorial assistant, which makes three of us on the editorial team.

Publishing two issues a year, do the three of you work on the magazine year round?

Yes, but we work on the website as well, so there's three people from an editorial standpoint that work on the magazine and the website full-time. A year ago my husband also published a magazine called *Jocks and Nerds*, which is a men's style magazine. At that time we decided that as we obviously do the same thing—his comes out four times a year while mine comes out twice—why not become one? So we started Tack Press together, which is the name of our publishing house. Tack Press publishes *Jocks and Nerds* and *Disegno*. Once we started that new enterprise a few more people joined the team, like Chris and Andrew who work in our sales department and on both of the magazines. Also, Anna works as a designer across the titles to help us with day-to-day things. So there are three people full-time and then I share three people with *Jocks and Nerds*.

Excellent. How long does it typically take for you to plan and put together an issue? Please briefly describe that process.

It takes about six months really. After going to print with one issue, we then sit down with all the sketches and ideas that we have for the next issue. I talk with the team about their ideas and what they have thought of and pinpoint

Perverted Fashion

Swedish fashion designer Ann-Sofie Back just won one of design's biggest prizes, but she's still cherishing obscurity.

WORDS Madelaine Levy
PHOTOS Ola Bergengren
STYLING and SET DESIGN Iwa Herdensjö

A flowchart of shoes by Ann-Sofie Back. From left to right, Swollen shoe S/S 2007, Square shoe S/S 2006, Wig shoe S/S 2004.

Photo by Ola Bergengren

the things that we're interested in exploring. It can be extremely vague at first, like a theme or something, or it could be that we saw loads of a specific product during different exhibitions and fairs. Or it could be that we noticed people using a new technique that we're interested in exploring. It might be that we saw one particular designer doing very well or showing a lot of product, and therefore would want to create a profile on them or something of that nature. So I guess it's about two months of basically having these vague ideas and notions, researching them, contacting people, asking contributors what they potentially would like to write about, and then formalizing that content into a mock-up flatplan. With the flatplan we know that the magazine is 208 pages every time and we know that a certain number are allocated for ad space, then we just say, "Okay, this story is probably going to be two pages and this story will probably be ten," and we just plan everything from there.

I think in general we have about twenty-four stories in every issue. I'd say about seven or eight of those are quite long, around three to five thousand words, and then the shorter ones are about one thousand to one thousand five hundred words. So we always know where the different divisions fall within the magazine.

Then it's a two-month period of commissioning, making sure that interviews are being set up, and that we're doing what we need to get those stories. *Disegno* has always made it a priority to go and experience the things that we write about; so we would never do an interview online or over the phone, as we like to do them in person. I allocate a certain budget for travel, to go see people or meet them in their studios or to go and see factories and things like that.

Next, ideally there would be a two-month period for editing and laying it all out. But I think all together it becomes about one month of editing and laying it out because often files are late or you're not happy and things need to be rewritten. In that last month we'll be working on the form and the design, editing and subediting, making sure to get it ready for print.

What would you say is the most challenging aspect of running a magazine?
For me, it's probably the fact that it's not just a magazine—it's also a business and I don't come from a business background. I don't have a business degree. I don't really know or have the formal tools for how a business is supposed to run. I am the director of that business as well as the editor in chief of the magazine, so I often find that I am split. I would love just to spend my time planning the magazine, but I have to spend a lot of time making sure that everything is running as it should, that people get paid on time and everyone is happy with what they are doing, that we're all working towards the same goal and so on. We have to work as a team in order to reach those end results so it's

important to make sure that everyone is on the same page.

When I started *Disegno* it was very solitary as it was just me sitting and working on the first issue, at times together with the art director. But you know I had a lot of freedom in terms of pursuing things, but now I have a team to look after and work with, so that often is the biggest challenge for me—feeling like I am three people instead of one.

And what's most rewarding? What makes you feel good about this venture?
Seeing the results. Seeing an issue come back from the printer that we've worked so hard on. To see that it's beautifully produced and that I'm happy with the colors and so on. Like the relaunch of the website today, getting used to it and seeing the benefits of the changes that we've made. So, yes seeing the results, and then as a side effect of that, of course, it's nice when people express their admiration for what you've done. I notice that as human beings we tend to take praise quite lightly but when something critical happens it kind of stays with us for a long time. I try not to base how happy I am about the magazine on people's attitudes or opinions about it because I don't think we can trust our own emotions to deal with that as well as we should.

I totally agree with you. Have you ever felt like giving up?
No. Once you start something like this, you can't really give up, because you're always trying to achieve something more or do something better. So just by making the decision to start the magazine, I always knew that it would be the kind of thing that I would continue doing for as long as I am able to. I'm hoping that there will be many more people involved in the future and that I'll be able to be a little freer with my time to maybe do other things like take a holiday. I hope that it will become more like a job instead of it being my whole life, but no, I don't think that it is something I would ever want to take a step back from. There is still so much more I want to achieve.

So it's definitely a labor of love?
Yes, definitely. Definitely.

What factors do you think contribute to a magazine's success?
I think the person's attitude toward the subject matters a whole lot. First and foremost I am very, very passionate about the subject of design. I think that's what I spend the most time thinking about in my daily life—how it benefits society and what impact it has for us as human beings in terms of how we live our lives. How we use things and how we can use objects, like how an iPhone [picks up Lorraine's iPhone] can impact the way you live your life [laughs], you know. Or how comfortable a chair is or how a pen is designed—how it sits in your hand. But it can also be how buses are designed or how roads are laid out or how bicycle parts are there or not there.

I just have to quickly ask, what's your favorite book on design that you've ever read?
My favorite book on design? I don't think I have one. The inspiration for *Disegno* in terms of the writing was always a book by a philosopher and linguist called Roland Barthes, a French writer who was active from the 1950s to the 1980s. The book is called *Mythologies* and it's a series of short observations about design and society.

But going back to your question, I think you have to have that passion for your topic because if you, for instance, start a magazine because you see a gap in the market, then it becomes more of a business opportunity where you're constantly worrying about the bottom line.

Ultimately, I don't think a successful magazine will necessarily be the best business idea, so I think it's always important to have that passion behind what you do—otherwise it can become really empty.

And what do you think contributes to failure?
Well, that would depend on what you see as success and failure. Some people think that making a lot of money means you are a big success, but for me the most important thing is to make things work. So I think that as long as you have people who are happy within the workplace and you can pay them their salaries, you can pay contributors their salaries, and so forth—but it doesn't mean that I have to be sitting in a big mansion somewhere. Just to have a healthy working kind of enterprise I think is a nice success, and it already takes a lot of work to get that to what it is.

I also think it's nice to have the respect from your peers and the people that you want to appeal to in terms of who reads the magazine, seeing that you've actually reached the audience you want to reach. I think that's very, very important. And again that comes back to this thing of some people will love it and some people will hate it, and some people will love it because they're featured in it, and some people will hate it because they're not [laughs].

So are you currently profitable?
Yes. It's actually interesting because this year for the first time we are looking at generating a small profit, whereas last year we just broke even.

Is your major revenue stream derived from a combination of both magazines?
Yes, it comes from the two magazines and the advertising sales in those magazines. We also have a side revenue stream from Tack Studio, which is creative agency work and is becoming much bigger for us. Due to the network of people we work with and our knowledge of our respective industries, we get asked by people to create aspects of their brand building such as advertising campaigns, or copywriting, or it could be contract publishing or other things along those lines. The income that we generate there is a big support in terms of how we work and grow as a business.

Disegno.

No.1

How do you go about attracting advertisers? How challenging is that?

I think you have to have a product that they want to be in in the first place. Then you need to be placed in the right stores so people know that you're out there, you have to make them aware of your presence. It's about being in people's field of vision and having a good ad sales team behind you too.

I don't think I'd ever be a good salesperson because it's not my strength, so Chris and Andrew, who are here, do it. They both have a long history of working in ad sales for other publications. That has been a very important step forward for the business. Before that, I had an agency that performed that particular duty. At that point I wasn't able to pay salaries so they took a percentage of what we earned. It's never the same when you don't work with someone who is in-house, because they can't fully communicate what you stand for and what the magazine is really about; plus they don't give you that much of their time.

What do you foresee for the magazine publishing industry in general? There is this battle about print and digital, which is getting rather boring now.

I think it's an old debate as well. I mean, we still have printed magazines, right? So I think there's still a very big interest in that medium. I also think that it will always be advantageous to have both an online and printed presence. For example, look at *Newsweek*, they went out

of print about two years ago and just went back into print because I presume that they didn't have as many subscribers and advertisers as they did when they were printing. So I feel there's still a very big focus on printed media.

Also, I think that most of our lives are spent staring at screens, surfing the internet, reading emails, and just living in the digital sphere in general. Having something that you can rest your eyes on that's printed and something you can touch, is a really nice experience; and I think that having a printed magazine really adds something for our readers.

What types of skills do you think are important for a magazine publisher to have?

That's a good question. I think that a lot of new magazines today are independently published so you definitely have to have the ability to multitask and focus on a lot of things at once. It's not necessarily about having the training in it because I don't think a lot of people do, but you must have the ability to take on board what it means for you to publish, like whether to print on one paper versus another. And you need to understand the lingo that printers speak, otherwise you will quickly stop communicating with them as a sector. So I think it's about being versatile and open-minded, listening to people, and not being scared to ask questions. We are three years down the line and I still learn lots of things every day. It's important to be open and not to feel like you need to know everything right from the start.

And my last question—what words of advice or encouragement do you have for a reader who's thinking about launching a publication?

Pursue it. It's something really exciting and something that makes me really happy to have done, but I think that it's very important to know where your passion lies and know exactly what your interest is. As I said, if it's about making money I don't think you will survive your first year because it's a really, really tough business—I think your passion needs to be for the subject matter rather than for anything else. Don't get me wrong, making a profit can be a happy side effect, but I don't think that's the thing it should be about from the start.

Philip Beesley DAM GALLERY Derivative Eno Henze Raquel Me

David OReilly Chris O'Shea Jer Thorp Semiconductor Zimoun

HOLO 1

HOLO

6

ALEXANDER SCHOLZ

Magazine name: *HOLO*
Founder and creative director: Alexander Scholz
Year founded: 2012 (first issue launched 2014)
Tagline: Emerging trajectories in art, science, and technology
Editorial mission: As consumer electronics become indistinguishable from science fiction, contemporary artists and designers are prototyping the future before our very eyes. *HOLO* takes the reader into their studios and workshops not only to discuss their work and understand their process, but to get some answers about the hyper-connected, technologically-accelerated present, where big cultural shifts can play out in a matter of months.
Location: Toronto, Canada; Berlin, Germany; London, UK
Website: holo-magazine.com
Format: Print only
Issues per year: Two
Language: English
Reach: Worldwide
Available: Website, digital newsstands, select independent booksellers, and magazine shops
Circulation: N/A
Price per issue: $35.00 USD
One-year subscription: $60.00 USD
Size of in-house team: Four part-time

Lorraine: Alex, so tell me, what were you doing before you launched *HOLO*?

Alex: I was busy making other magazines—I have a publishing background and have been working over the past decade as an art director and writer for several publications that dealt with arts, culture, and technology. *SCEEN* is probably one worth mentioning—it was a DVD-equipped digital arts and culture magazine, that I founded, designed, and edited back in the mid-2000s.

So what made you decide to go back into publishing again?

I never really got over the fact that I had to let *SCEEN* go because it was not sustainable at the time. I threw all my money at it but unfortunately it never made anything back.

Although there's no comparison with *HOLO*, *SCEEN* actually dealt with similar topics and I never stopped believing that there was an ongoing need for a publication just like it. When I moved to Toronto in 2009 (I lived in Hamburg, Germany before) I felt that the time was right to give it another shot so I slowly began development of my idea and was constantly on the lookout for like-minded peers.

I found them over at CreativeApplications. Net—it was a new, popular blog that covered the same topical milieu. I joined them as a regular contributor but quickly realized that the magazine I was working on would make an ideal companion to the blog—a more enduring extension that would allow us to expand our online offering. We realized that if we wanted to tell different stories then we would need to move away from the web and look at a medium that would allow people to step away from their screens and engage with our content in a totally different way.

Did you do any market research prior to launching or was this just something in your heart that you went with?

Our CreativeApplications.Net blog attracted about 300,000 visitors a month, so we knew there was an audience out there and predicted that it could only get bigger as young people nowadays grow up with technology—it's the tool of our time. Most students learn how to code in university; they learn how to use cutting-edge technology to create art, to design things, you know, to kind of interrogate how we look at the world.

Although we knew we had an audience, we didn't necessarily know whether they would "get" a print magazine on the subject, as well as be willing to spend money on it. To test the waters, we shared a preview booklet of the magazine with artists, curators, and peers that we selected from within our field. All of them loved it, but that wasn't a guarantee for us as in order to make a magazine work you need "critical mass."

So why Kickstarter?

It was the only way to fund the magazine. We had pitched *HOLO* to a good number of international arts and design publishers—Gestalten in Berlin, Frame Publishers in Amsterdam, and the Princeton Architectural Press in New York—but nobody was willing to take a chance on us. I still remember Robert Klanten of Gestalten telling me that a new magazine would need years of major investment before it could make any money and that it just wasn't a good time for print. I was devastated. As our editor in chief, Greg Smith, used to say, "We're all dressed up but have nowhere to go."

We didn't allow our heads to hang for too long though, as we'd already worked extensively on the first issue and at that point nobody was willing to give up. As a matter of fact, we felt strangely emboldened by the rejection and concluded that if we wanted to make the magazine exactly the way we wanted it to be, then we'd have to do it ourselves, and that meant going in all the way—creating the content as well as publishing the actual magazine. Kickstarter was still pretty new back in spring 2012, but it seemed to be the right tool to use to ask our blog readers and others for their support in financing our first issue.

I saw that your goal for funding was originally $35,000 but you ended up managing to double that. Was the original amount you calculated an estimate of what you thought it would cost to just produce the first issue?

Yes, the $35,000 was the bare minimum we figured we'd need to get that first issue printed. The number was based on our initial calculations from all the quotes we had received from both the printers and distributors. That number turned out to be far off, because *HOLO* 1 ended up having many more pages and contributors than we had initially intended. We were very lucky that we surpassed our funding goal the way we did.

Deciding on that magic number is an extremely tricky thing—set the goal too low and you risk ending up coming up short, set it too high and you take the risk of receiving nothing at all. I'm sure we could have published that first issue for $35,000 but it would have been a totally different magazine.

How did it feel when you received that kind of response?

Oh my goodness—it was overwhelming in every sense of the word, we simply couldn't believe what was happening. We reached our funding goal within five days of the campaign. I'm still amazed that our supporters—most of whom are "digital natives" and at home on the web—immediately got it, and enthusiastically pledged for a print magazine in late 2012. Many people responded and said, "I am so glad that somebody's finally doing this. I've been looking forward to reading a magazine like this for years." That was such a relief and an encouragement.

Refreshing our Kickstarter page became a bit of an obsession for us during those days. The moment the campaign was over I remember our project manager, Sherry Kennedy, writing on our Skype team channel, "I am so happy that I want to cry!" and that's how we all felt.

We had all sacrificed so much for the project already that the campaign became a make-or-break moment. Let's not forget that putting an idea on Kickstarter also means risking public failure. We had no backup plan either, and not reaching our goal could have meant the end of *HOLO* for good.

How did you arrive at the name *HOLO* for the magazine?

Picking a name was really difficult, but I think what finally drew us to *HOLO* was the long history of the word (it's Greek and means "whole") and its use in retro tech and science fiction contexts. Holograms, holography, and holodecks have been around in literature, film, and TV for decades now and have always been associated with a fantastical future that's yet to come. To this day, holograms haven't left the prototype stage. This notion of anticipating the future seemed like a great fit with the editorial mandate of the magazine.

So your initial vision for the magazine was about expanding the vision of the blog in a way that you couldn't do online?

Yeah, I mean, we love the immediacy of the web and speed is great for skimming and sharing, but the attention span is just not there—and it's just not ideal for extensive, more involved stories, especially for a niche blog like ours. There just isn't any money to do something other than discussing new works or running the occasional email interview or essay. A great feature requires months of research, possibly travel, and either professional photography or illustration—nothing our blog could afford to do or that would last long in what is such a fast-paced, ephemeral medium.

Philip Beesley ——— p.170

We also became more and more frustrated with the growing staleness within the general art and design blogosphere—the same polished press images, videos, and rehashed artist statements everywhere! No substance, no process, no discourse.

Rather than contribute to that trend, we wanted to show the people behind the works that we were excited about, the environments they were created in, the artistic positions and processes that drove them, and with *HOLO* we finally got to do that. The magazine was not only a way for us to slow down and reflect and put the things that we see on the web into perspective, it also allowed us to step into the places where "the magic" actually happens and that's inside the artists' studios.

What really sets your magazine apart from others that are out there then?
First I have to mention that there are other great periodicals that cover similar terrain—for instance, there's MIT Press' *Leonardo Music Journal* and *Neural Computation*, which have both been around for decades. We have the highest regard for both these publications, but their writing is very much on the academic side and speaks mostly to knowledgeable insider circles. For us, it was important to make *HOLO* accessible to a broader audience and in some small way, help to make sense of all the societal uncertainties about our present time that's so hyper-connected and technology-accelerated.

Who is the magazine aimed at?
Any type of curious creative really—artists, architects, designers, illustrators, programmers, or even researchers. We certainly make the magazine with a broad range in mind. But *HOLO* definitely has a core readership of creative coders, media artists, interaction designers, experimental filmmakers, people who create work at the intersection of art, science, and technology. "Hybrid Heroes," as Golan Levin, the media artist, calls them. We put a lot of work into making the magazine as interesting to them as to the "freshmen" that just want to catch a glimpse into this world.

I'm listening to you and it sounds like you have a really nice cross section, whether you're a coder or a designer, because I'm a coder and a designer and you're right—there's nothing out there that speaks to me. It's either about code or it's about design and rarely are the two subjects delivered together, so I totally understand where you're coming from. How did you attract readers starting out? I know you had the blog and Kickstarter gave you a lot of publicity—but what about other vehicles, how important was social media?
All those things were really important. The blog was well established so its network and social media channels were available to us and that certainly made the biggest difference. It was interesting that the visibility on Kickstarter helped us attract new readers even long after the campaign had ended.

During all those long months of editorial production the successful campaign functioned like a sales pitch for *HOLO* that had people reaching out to us every other day about pre-ordering. I must say, even though it was shot at four in the morning after forty-eight sleepless hours of setup and prep, the campaign video made a pretty decent case for a magazine that is really not that easy to pitch at all.

How did you wind up getting distribution on that first issue?

We knew from our Kickstarter data that *HOLO*'s audience was truly international, with readers from North and South America, Europe, Asia, and Australia. That meant that shipping costs were going to be a big part of the overall equation. Unfortunately, international shipping from North America turned out to be very expensive, so expensive in fact that it would have jeopardized the entire operation. Luckily—thanks to a lot of research and some friendly advice from fellow indie publishers—we soon found out that Deutsche Post in Germany, my home country, had shockingly competitive rates.

Really?

Yes, it was close to half of what we would have paid out of America. Many other small publishers had come to the same conclusion as us. The distributor we ended up working with in Berlin ships some of the best international indie magazines, and none of them are based in Germany. A visit to their facilities is like going to a really well curated magazine shop.

How easy was it for you to get distribution?

Pretty easy. As I said, our distributor was already working with other independent magazines like ours and knew exactly what we needed. We gave him a weight and size estimate and he came back to us with a quote. Then we calculated the shipping budget and set aside the funds. Once *HOLO* was printed, the entire run went straight to the distributor where our inventory is stored, packaged, and fulfilled according to our wishes. Once a week we send the new orders that have come from our online shop or the stockists that we deal with individually, and they take care of the rest. It's pretty straightforward and allows us to keep our focus on making a really great magazine.

Feel free not to answer, but what was the number of your initial print run?

That's fine, we're very open about that—5,000 copies. That doesn't sound like much, but given the book-ish production quality and size— *HOLO* 1 is just over 220 pages and comes with an extra 20-page booklet—that's quite an expensive undertaking. The number of 5,000 turned out to be a good choice by the way as we're now more than 80 percent sold out and hope to increase our run for issue two.

It's been documented that a lot of magazines don't typically make a profit until year two or three, if they even manage to make it past that

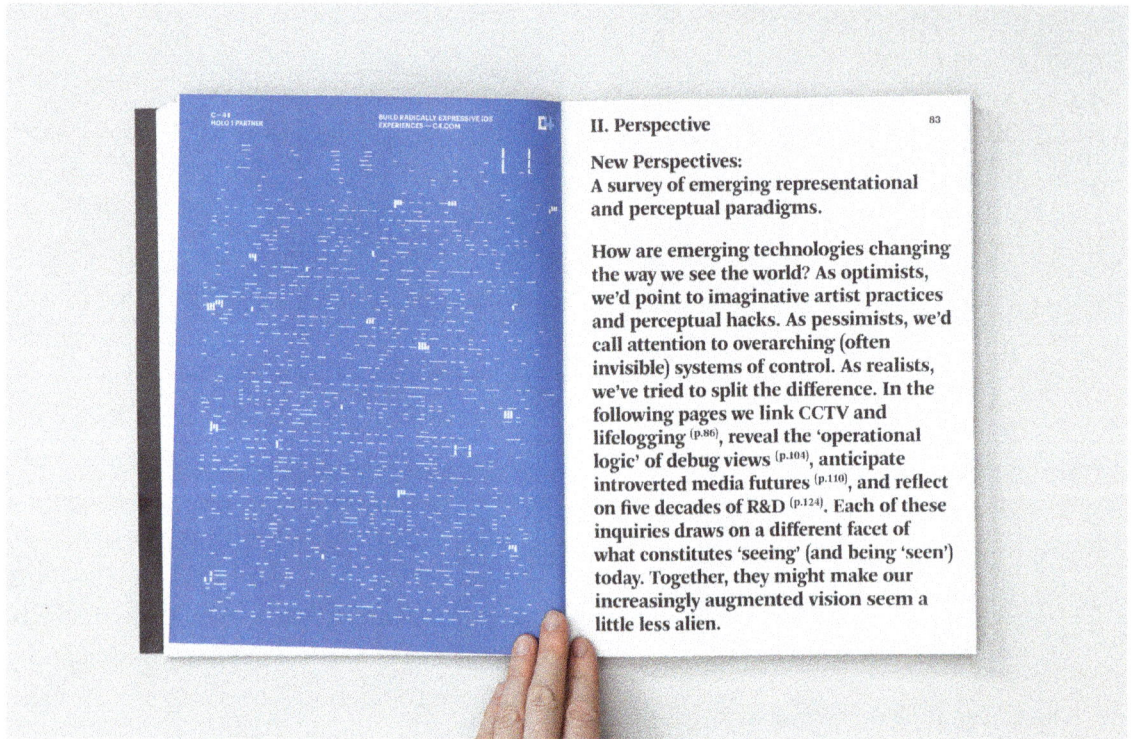

first year. **Is it possible that you might start profiting in your first year, or do you predict that it will be much later on down the line?**

HOLO is definitely a long game. We survived the first year without going broke and hope to turn a small profit with issue two. But it will be a while before this venture will be sustainable enough that we can compensate ourselves for the hours we put in every day. We all have gigs on the side to pay the bills. We do compensate our contributors though—writers, photographers, illustrators, and designers—and have done so since day one. I think it's an important part of being taken seriously as a professional publication and building those necessary sustainable relationships.

How many people do you have working in-house?

We're a really small team. It's really just four people that run the entire operation, including the blog CreativeApplications.Net. And we're not really "in-house" either, as we're scattered all around the world. There's Filip Visnjic, our London-based editorial director. Greg Smith, the editor in chief, and Sherry Kennedy, our project manager, who are both in Toronto. And then there's me, and I'm now back in Berlin. So that's it!

We have a large roster of external contributors though—photographers, journalists, illustrators, and guest designers. I believe the total number of people that worked with us on issue one is thirty-five.

It looks as if it took about a year and a half for you to complete that first issue. Were you working out the kinks—what it would look like, what content it would contain and so on?
The first issue was largely mapped out when the Kickstarter campaign came to a close. The fact that it still took us about eighteen months—about a year longer than anticipated—to finish *HOLO* 1 was due to several reasons.

One is that the finer details of becoming a publisher—which is very different from making a magazine—took quite some time to resolve. Another is that we had to start the design process three times over thanks to bad luck with some of our contractors. And finally, the Kickstarter aftermath was an utter time sink.

People think that setting up the campaign, shooting a video, and spreading the word is the hard part. The truth is that nobody prepares you for the horrors of administration once the campaign is over. From composing regular campaign updates, to organizing, producing, and shipping all the additional rewards we gave—for us, Kickstarter seemed to never end. We used to joke that we started out wanting to make a magazine but ended up gift wrapping instead.

[Laughs] Right.
And I haven't even discussed keeping about

a thousand shipping addresses of backers all over the world up to date. Yes, I'm glad our Kickstarter days are over.

Please briefly describe the process from planning the table of contents to completing the final layout, or is the magazine so new that a process hasn't really been defined as of yet?
Work on issue one was definitely a somewhat erratic, if not messy, process that involved many bumps and detours. We had the different sections and large parts of the content pretty much figured out from early on, but with no template to work from and three of us never having worked on a publication before, we all had our own idea or vision of what *HOLO* would eventually become.

Compared to issue one, work on number two is going pretty smoothly. We've all grown into our roles and simply know how the magazine works now. We began with selecting the featured artists and matching them with the right journalists and photographers. Once studio visits were locked down, we started filling the other magazine sections, the most laborious one probably being the thematic "idea" section, which takes up a good third of the magazine.
The design comes last, although it's my job as the creative director to develop the content with the design in mind. After a first design pass, editing on the page begins, which is a tedious process that can take up to two months. From the first decisions up until publishing, we're probably looking at about six months.

Six months? Okay. I was fascinated with the cover of the first issue. Can you explain how that came about and what exactly it is? It was just so genuine, so unique—just brilliant.
Thanks! As you can imagine, the decision of what goes on the cover of your very first issue can be terrifying, especially when the magazine's tagline reads "emerging trajectories in art, science, and technology"—how do you capture that in one image?

The idea was that we don't really believe in a fixed logo being tied to the magazine. So stepping away from some of the standard things that you would associate with a publication —like how you would build a brand and so forth—we kind of wanted to reinvent the magazine for each issue. So in search of something new and radical, we turned to Luna Maurer and Jonathan Puckey of the design studio Moniker, that's based in Amsterdam.

With their help we developed a conditional design system that considered all the letters on every page in our magazine and traced all the occurrences of the letters in our name—H, O, and L—throughout the entire issue. The results were then used to render an intricate distribution map. So the pixel burst you see on the cover is essentially an abstract representation of the magazine's content as represented by the letters in our name—which is not only unique but, I think, adds a very nice touch as well.

Did you use a particular software to generate the visualization map or did you have it specially coded?

We used Processing which is a very accessible programming environment that was developed with artists in mind. It was a natural choice for us because it's free, open source, has a huge community, and is perfect for playing around, experimenting, and prototyping ideas. It's no surprise that so many digital artists use it today. Just search for "Processing" on our blog and you'll see all the amazing projects that have been created with it.

I was just thinking that now you have to find a way to outdo yourself for issue two.
I know! Fortunately we've already picked the guest designer who will work with us on the cover of *HOLO* 2. In fact, we're having our first Skype call today—let's see if we can top the cover of our first issue.

Well, good luck with that.
Thank you.

What do you find most challenging about running *HOLO*?
Keeping the ship afloat with an international team of four is challenging to this day. Ever since the magazine came out we also have to deal with distribution, marketing, stockists, and press every day. Only half of all the hours that we put into the project account for work on the actual magazine—at best. Fortunately we embraced all the duties that come with being a publisher and work pretty well as a team. On the less practical end of the spectrum, the biggest challenge is probably meeting our own high standards. We haven't exactly picked an easy mandate—many of the things we consider

"emerging trajectories in art, science, and technology" are fairly new and little explored. And we aren't necessarily always the experts either. To add something meaningful to the discourse between art and science and comment on all the implications of ubiquitous computer technology requires a lot of thought, research, and above all, time.

What do you find to be the most rewarding as far as publishing the magazine?

Nothing beats seeing the enthusiasm of our readers. Once the first issue was finally headed out around the world, there was this wave of magazine selfies that all our happy recipients shared on Facebook, Twitter, and Instagram, along with comments like, "Yay, I finally got my copy!" After working in a bubble for eighteen months it was really electrifying to finally see people respond to the result with so much excitement—eight months later, the pictures still keep coming in! It was also fantastic to read the glowing reviews and to see the magazine at our favorite magazine stand and design bookstore.

What factors do you think contribute to the success of a magazine? Being so new you're obviously looking at those factors with regards to your own publication.

To me, a good magazine is one that matters. And to matter means to produce content a reader cares deeply about and just can't get anywhere else. That means knowing your audience

and offering something they won't find on the likes of Tumblr, Instagram, or Pinterest. That's why many publications of general interest and broader culture struggle. Nobody needs yet another magazine that just runs a safe mix of art, design, music, architecture, fashion, and lifestyle—trust me, the web has got you covered on that.

Would you say it's the opposite of that that contributes to failure then, not knowing your audience or understanding what they want?
Yeah, I think so. It's just as important to know who you're talking to—or at least want to talk to—as it is to know what you're talking about.

Going back to revenue and advertising, you have an interesting ad sales strategy. Can you explain that?
Sure. Our partnership program, as we call it, was a creative response to the initial advertisements we received for *HOLO* 1. Some of them were decent, others were just plain ugly. Most of our advertisers were from our immediate editorial universe—digital arts festivals, arts organizations, small media labs, and research institutions—and half of them had never designed an ad before. We were in a tough spot: on the one hand we wanted these organizations to look good—after all, we love what they do—on the other hand we didn't have the time to design individual ads for them.

I never really liked the idea of running regular ads anyway. At best an ad is perceived as a disruptive necessity, and this wasn't how we wanted these organizations to be seen. So we started thinking about ways to elevate their role and integrate them more seamlessly into the magazine. Once we thought of them not as advertisers but as partners, it all fell into place.

We went back to square one and invited them to participate in a design experiment, where we would use the same system that generated the magazine cover for a series of dedicated partner pages. So instead of the letters H, O, L, we visualized all the occurrences of the letters in our partners' names. The result was a really nice sequence of different distribution maps running through the magazine that, technically and conceptually, connected each partner to all the content in the issue—which speaks quite nicely to the idea of partnership, I think. And in addition to the partner pages we also introduced each partner editorially—what they do and why they are awesome—in the intro section of the magazine.

Interesting. So what skills or disciplines do you think are important for a magazine publisher to have today?
I would say a good combination of editorial instinct and entrepreneurial savviness. You have to love and understand the medium, you have to have a nose for good stories and ideas about how to tell them. You shouldn't be averse to administration and bookkeeping either. Oh, and you should know how to work the web too. Because that's where you'll meet and engage

with your readers. Generally, the more versatile you are the better, especially in small operations like ours where very few people have to do many different things.

What last words of advice would you offer someone who may be considering launching their own publication?

I would say keep at it! It's never been easier to launch a print publication than it is today—largely thanks to the web, ironically. Magazine makers can find their readers online, build an audience, sell copies directly, and operate largely independent from twentieth-century necessities like publishers, newsstands, or distributors. You can literally start a magazine alone and from your bedroom. Having said that, with all the content available for free online, you'll have to work extra hard to convince people to buy and keep buying your magazine. So be bold, be brave, be different—good magazines will always be in demand.

And lastly, don't let setbacks get to you. If we had known about some of the challenges we had coming our way we'd probably have given up halfway through, but we didn't. It's sweet, innocent optimism that kept us going until we finally came through. So keep going!

So you're basically saying that a little bit of ignorance is bliss.

Oh yes, absolutely!

IdN

International designers' Network

VOLUME 21 NO. 1

EFFECTS SPECIAL

FEATURE:

The Printed Matter Its tactile qualities, even the sound and smell of paper and ink, make printed matter unique and timeless. 14 experts show how various effects make print matters.

amazing 60 projects

14 dESIGNERS

• Anonymous • Büro Für Design • Confetti Studio • ENZED • Maria Fischer • Yurko Gutsulyak • Homework • Kolektiv Studio • Munsure • CWT Creative/Jon Hannan • Tommy Perez • RoAndCo • Joe Shouldice • Work In Progress

---

UNIQUE PAPER STOCK
SPECIAL INKS METALLICS
VARNISHES SPOT COLORS
HEAT SENSITIVE FOLDING
STITCH BINDING SCORING
PERFORATION DIE CUTTING
LAZER ETCHING EMBOSSING
FOIL STAMPING
LETTERPRESSING
SCREENPRINTING
AND MORE •••

CREATIVE COUNTRY:

URUGUAY

Small but Perfectly Formed – Taking a look at the modern design scene in one of South America's smallest countries: Uruguay

ALSO IN THIS ISSUE:

Studio: All About Aesthetics Supermundane / Des Signes / Index Studio / Ariane Spanier / Trapped in Suburbia

Glitch / Art of the Imperfect: Irina Kopytina / Design Reform Council / Tyler Spangler / Fanakalo

+ MOTION GALLERY:

SEEMLESS TRANSITION

Three leading exponents of making seamless transition work — 18Bis, Golden Wolf and Masanobu Hiraoka — share the secrets of their magic touch. + 15 more studios showcasing their profolios with flawless transistions.

IdN

LAURENCE NG

Magazine name: *IdN* (*International designers' Network*)
Founder and publisher: Laurence Ng
Year founded: 1992
Tagline: Wider resources for creative professionals
Editorial mission: To amplify and unify the design community
Location: Hong Kong
Website: idnworld.com
Format: Print only
Issues per year: Six
Languages: English and traditional Chinese
Reach: Worldwide
Available: Website, digital newsstands, newsstands, and bookstores
Circulation: 90,000 combined
Price per issue: $19.95 USD
One-year subscription: $118 USD (Includes 6 regular issues and 1 IdNPRO publication)
Size of in-house team: Nine (one publisher, one art director, one editor, one features editor, one designer, one production manager, one circulation manager, one subscriptions manager, and one sh** kicker)

Lorraine: Hi Laurence, what did you do before launching your magazine?
Laurence: I provided graphic arts services.

How did you get into magazine publishing? Where did the idea come from?
The magazine started as an experiment in digital publishing.

Did you do any market research or create a business plan prior to launching?
No, there was no market research or business plan. It was the early '90s and at that time everything you did had a potential market somewhere out there.

Knowing what you know now, do you think it's important to create a plan or some type of road map when starting out?
It's more important to understand that being involved with independent media isn't a job or a career—it's a way of life.

How did you initially go about funding your magazine?
Advertisers funded the early offerings of *IdN*. People were and still are the most important investment. Logistics is also a huge part of your overall expense.

What was your initial vision for the magazine? Has that changed any?
Starting out, *IdN* was more about the technology behind print, now it's more about design and creative cultures.

In what way do you think *IdN* is different from the competition? What sets your magazine apart from others who cover the same subject matter?
We use various print techniques and different paper stock in each issue. It's as much about showcasing the design and the creators as it is about the print industry in general.

IdN

International
designers
Network

FEATURE:

VOLUME21 NO. 3
EDITORIAL
ILLUSTRATION

NEW FACES OF INSPIRATION

Editorial illustration is more than just an added extra
to give a page of dense type eye-appeal – it can
actually add significantly to the interpretation of a story,
especially if it features a face. We asked 10 specialists
to share their trade secrets with us.

- ANDREW ARCHER
- PAUL BLOW
- MILES DONOVAN
- SAM FALCONER
- DAVID FOLDVARI
- PAUL X. JOHNSON
- MUM
- RAMI NIEMI
- CHRIS TSEVIS
- JOE WILSON

CREATIVE COUNTRY:
FINLAND

Is this northern European Nordic
country still a reference point for
contemporary designers?

+ MOTION GALLERY:
I WANT MY MTV

Enjoy 90 minutes of non-stop motion video
artistry by 18 leading units. All of them
interview the studios in the book and tell us
why they love the genre and where they think
its future lies. Chic & Artists / Motion Theory
/ Paul Trillo / Beauty Ohms

ALSO IN THIS ISSUE:

Playable Graphic Design
Board games by Rodpunkt and Lee Wan
Yee / Designer Calendars by Peter von
Freihold and Kafis Petiter / Interactive
publication by Koh Min Yu

Studios: Branded Identity
Transwhite / Ordinary People
/ Matt Luckhurst / Novelkp

What does your audience look like? Who reads *IdN*?
It's about 40 percent graphic designers and 16 percent students and educators, then smaller percentages of web and multimedia designers, art directors, creative directors, illustrators, etc.

Starting out, how did you find readers?
We simply carried the magazines in our suitcases and traveled to bookstores and newsstands around the world.

What can you tell us about distribution? How did you start and do you have a plan or partners that are responsible for that?
Finding distributors is not rocket science but it takes a lot of persistence to partner with the right ones. International book fairs like the ones held in Frankfurt and London are good locations for carrying out research.

How long does it take for you to plan and put together an issue?
We run bimonthly and our cycles are typically two months.

Briefly describe the process from planning the table of contents to completing the final layout of an issue.
We start with a blank page each time and take it from there.

What technologies do you use in publishing the magazine?
We use InDesign, Photoshop, and Illustrator.

What types of interactivity or forms of multimedia do you use?
We stream our video content online.

Has mobile affected or changed the way you do business?
It's made it harder—information now is almost worthless because it's so easy to obtain online.

What's the most challenging part of running a magazine?
Balance sheets!

What's the most rewarding part of running your magazine?
Inspiring others.

Have you ever felt like giving it up?
Yes, but we didn't give up because some people have been with us for over twenty years.

What factors do you think contributes to the success of a magazine in general?
The size of your team.

And what about its failure?
Also the size of your team.

What indicators or metrics do you use to gauge the success or growth of your audience and readership?
Sales figures.

Are you currently profitable?
No.

How soon do you expect to see a profit for your magazine?

We don't foresee a profitable future for independent print publications of our type but we are aiming to run a balance this year.

Briefly describe how you go about setting a budget for the magazine.

Only spend if you have to, otherwise save it.

What are your major revenue streams right now and which streams are you focused on growing?

Newsstand sales and subscriptions.

Can you tell us a little bit about your ad sales strategy?

We don't have a strategy because we don't rely on income from advertisers.

What do you foresee for the magazine publishing industry in general?

Go big. Either be a large multi-national or go independently small. Everything else in between will burn.

What skills or disciplines do you think are important for a magazine publisher of today to have?

Opinions.

What last message of wisdom or inspiration would you like to leave our readers who may be considering launching a publication?

Know your topic well. To compete, printed magazines will have to be more and more specialized and niche.

An international selection of
design, people and business
N_1
Fall 2011
HEROINE

KATACHI

KEN OLLING

Magazine name: *Katachi*
Founder and CEO: Ken Olling
Year founded: 2010
Tagline: An international selection of design, people, and business
Editorial mission: To create interactive, timeless content that is not contemporary or of a particular moment
Location: Oslo, Norway
Website: katachimag.com
Format: Interactive/digital (iPad only)
Issues per year: Three
Languages: English, Japanese, and Norwegian
Reach: Worldwide
Available: Apple's App Store
Downloads: 100,000 (over a three-year period)
Price per issue: $2.99 USD
Subscription prices: $5.99 and $10.99 USD
Size of in-house team: Fourteen full-time and ten freelance

Lorraine: Hi Ken, can you tell me what you did before launching your digital magazine?
Ken: Yes, I previously worked as a graphic designer and a brand consultant.

How did the idea for *Katachi* come about?
The 2010 SXSW—which is the big music, film, and interactive festival—took place just weeks before the iPad first launched. We were excited about it and went to all the presentations that had anything to do with interactive publishing. After seeing that most of the presenters were talking about this as just another channel, we had some beers and decided that we did not agree—so we set out to create our own magazine with a modest goal—to publish the most interactive magazine in the world.

As of 2013, we were being awarded App of the Year at SPD 48 in New York and Best Digital Magazine at DMA in London in competition with some of the best and biggest publishers out there. As a self-funded start-up from Oslo, this was quite a feat.

And let me clarify—by "just another channel" I'm talking about the way traditional media outlets treat publishing today, in that you design and make content once, usually for print, and then just make "replica editions" for all other channels like web, mobile, or tablet. We believe that if content would be better in print or on the web, then we don't put it into our digital magazine—plain and simple.

Did you do any market research prior to launching your digital magazine? With the medium being so new that must have been next to impossible to do.
We didn't do any market research because we felt that our approach was better. We did create a business plan, but since this was before anything had launched on the iPad, there was no real data to work from, just assumptions from

similar things. We had a limited budget and just had to work with what we had.

Do you still use any of that original documentation today?

No, not at all. Pretty much everything about it has been completely changed several times and our business plan has pivoted at least three times. Katachi Media is a service provider and a software company as well as a publishing company—and that's just the beginning.

Knowing what you know now, do you think it's important to create a plan or some type of road map when starting out?

It would be impossible to know all the things that we know now, but a plan is never completely wasted. I think rather than spend a lot of time on an ever-changing business plan, it would be better to spend time and resources on an aggressive marketing plan. Magazines are appealing and interesting, but they are hard to find. For instance, Newsstand is generally a place where good magazines go to die, so a way of being found in the different app stores is something very important to consider.

How did you select your magazine's name?

We wrote a list of about fifteen different names with the vision of a magazine that we would find interesting and *Katachi* happened to be one of these. The others were quite abstruse but still had meaning. First we looked at whether these names had existed recently as magazines, and most of them had. For us the name had to

easily roll off your tongue, be memorable, and most importantly it needed to have an available URL. Katachi.com was taken, so we ended with katachimag.com. Katachi means "form" or "shape" in Japanese and there was actually a *Katachi Magazine* back in the '70s, but we felt that it was far back enough for us to go ahead and use it.

How did you initially go about funding your magazine?

The first round was basically self-funded with some additional help and investment from family and friends. That said, we are always looking for investors, but as we've managed to come this far we are only interested in entertaining the *right* investor.

What was your initial vision for the magazine? Has that changed any?

The vision was to create the most interactive magazine in the world and no, that vision has not changed. The way we approached this new medium was to have access to a set of tools that allowed us to create a unique, interactive experience. Since this happened parallel to the launch of the iPad itself, there was nothing out there tool-wise for us to use, so we ended up building it ourselves—that is when Origami Engine™ was born.

Initially it was meant just as a tool for creating *Katachi Magazine,* but it has since become our core business and we are licensing it to students, designers, magazine publishers, and even enterprises all over the world that have been searching for a tool that could help them create unique interactive experiences. So although the vision for the magazine has not changed, the vision for Katachi Media has.

Who is your digital magazine aimed at?

We did not really have a specific target audience although we did want a fifty-fifty split of men and women. That said, it's not a magazine for all. The content is not necessarily alienating, but it is definitely ahead of the curve as far as interactive elements. The need to communicate a message has always been the core for the choice of interaction and the amount of it. But the fact that it's a brand new way of experiencing media in this way means that it most probably resonates the most with the early adopters of Apple, and of course inquisitive designers as well.

Starting out, how did you attract readers? What did you do both online and offline to reach them?

When *Katachi Magazine* no. 1 "HEROINE," came out in November 2011, we had a well-deserved small launch party here in Oslo. We also did our best to spread the word with Facebook, Twitter, and Instagram. Having limited means meant that our reach was also limited, so people usually found us because we were one of the very few real interactive magazines out there. Because they found *Katachi* beautiful, interesting, fun, and even confusing at times, they began to tweet and write about it.

And the fact that we've won quite a few awards has increased our visibility tremendously.

We should have been better at marketing, but we're a tiny organization and we were extremely busy finishing work on the tool, as well as preparing for our next issue. But once again, we'd have made better use of our time focusing more on a marketing plan than an ever-changing business plan.

What do you do now to find new readers and subscribers? What do you find to be effective—your website?

Yes, somewhat important, but the iTunes App Store is still quite a way from it. When a user comes to a website they have to go through a lot of steps before actually buying the magazine. We see that every click you introduce between looking for and buying the app or magazine means the more people that you lose in the process. For instance, Twitter > Website > Link > App Store > Bookshelf > Issue > Buy stand-alone issue versus Twitter > Link > App Store > Buy stand-alone issue. It's important to have a website, but for us, sales are not made first and foremost from our site.

Blog?

Yes, it's important, but we're not very good at using it.

Social media?

We use Facebook, Twitter, and Instagram as time allows, which is daily more often than not.

It is the hardest to decipher among the Guerlain family.
To articulate it's self-restraint and dilemma Jacques Gu
committing it to a state of flux. The angular qualities

SCENT

and out of consciousness, the picture never becomes clear.
loped a cacophony of citrus, sweet, wood and musk cyphre
uous nature lends itself to be an androgynous perfume.

ISIONS

O
AS
N
THE
T SO
ONE
HAT
RLAIN
RING
LIST
.

What do you think is more important, your website or social media, and why?

Social media is more important than your website. Sharing, along with social shares, Facebook likes, and general recommendations from people you know, seems to be the best ways of getting access to new audiences. The personal hook is better than a promoted slogan. Being written about in a positive context—things like winning awards—is also a great way of being introduced.

SEO?

Not done much.

Email marketing?

Yes, we do this regularly in order to keep our users informed.

Content marketing?

Not used.

Traditional marketing like radio, TV, flyers, brochures, etc.?

Not used.

Why did you decide to go digital only?

Print is a fantastic medium, but digital is a medium in and of itself. In my opinion, trying to mix the two would take them both in the wrong direction. We wanted to completely innovate in the digital space, and having a print tag-along would have hindered us in the process.

What can you tell me about your experience of selling through the App Store on iTunes?

When we first launched, the first ten pages of the magazine was free. The conversion rate at that time was as low as 25 percent. Once we got rid of the free part, conversions increased to 80 percent. This number was greatly influenced by those who had already purchased our first issue. If we had to do it again, however, we probably would do it differently.

Another interesting aspect of selling through the App Store is that sales are incremental, not cyclical, so each time we publish a new edition, we sell more of the old ones, too. This element of longevity is a new aspect in magazine publishing and should influence the way you think about making content less time-sensitive.

How did you go about actually creating and designing the magazine, including reimagining content for an interactive device?

We ask important questions like, "Would this be better in print?" If yes, then we don't do it. Or we ask, "Would this be better on the web?" If yes, then we don't do that either. If we still feel that the communicative suggestions we are coming up with are good, interactive ideas that create new and interesting experiences, only then do we move forward. As a result we throw a ton of ideas away.

How do you embellish the publication— what types of interactivity do you use?

[Laughs] "Embellish" would already be in violation of our communication starting points mentioned above. When we decide on a design concept we use what interactive elements we need to communicate that idea. If it does not exist, we make it. This is the reason why we made Origami Engine™ in the first place. Also, having the tool sets us apart from publishers who have to work within the limitations of their accessible toolbox.

Do you ever have an idea for the magazine that the tool is not yet able to deliver, how do you handle or work around that?
Yes, perpetually. But as I mentioned, we're probably better off than most in this case, since we're deciding on our own tool's future features and functionality. That said, a tool will always be limiting in that it only has a set number of uses. Origami Engine™ has had the focus of giving the designer a more granular set of tools—most of the elements can be combined together in a way that creates almost infinite possibilities for the user.

What other tools do you use for *Katachi* other than Origami Engine™?
We use all the standard design tools like Photoshop, Illustrator, Sketch, PaintCode, 3D software, After Effects, and Lightroom.

What experience do you intend to provide for a reader? What should they get out of your interactive magazine?
A greater insight into the editorial content and an experience that leaves a memorable impression. We think in terms of "layers" of content. A core editorial story should never be hidden, but there will be a reward if you as a reader are willing to spend time exploring around the pages. You won't miss anything if you don't go looking, but if you do you'll get an additional and often a more emotional feeling to the story when you take the time to detect or discover the additional interactivity.

What do you find to be the most challenging part of running a digital magazine?
The production of proper interactive content is very challenging and time-consuming and requires a great deal of creativity and innovation. A lot of this has to do with having no examples to show or explain what you are looking for. This has become better of course, but when we started out it was a real problematic issue. In addition, general funding, finding advertisers, and subsequently having time and money for marketing are all challenging aspects of being a start-up.

What is the most rewarding part of running a digital magazine for you?
When people copy what we do, we see that we've definitely brought something concrete to the conversation. We believe that *Katachi* has influenced the direction of interactive magazines positively—moving them away from the standard PDF.

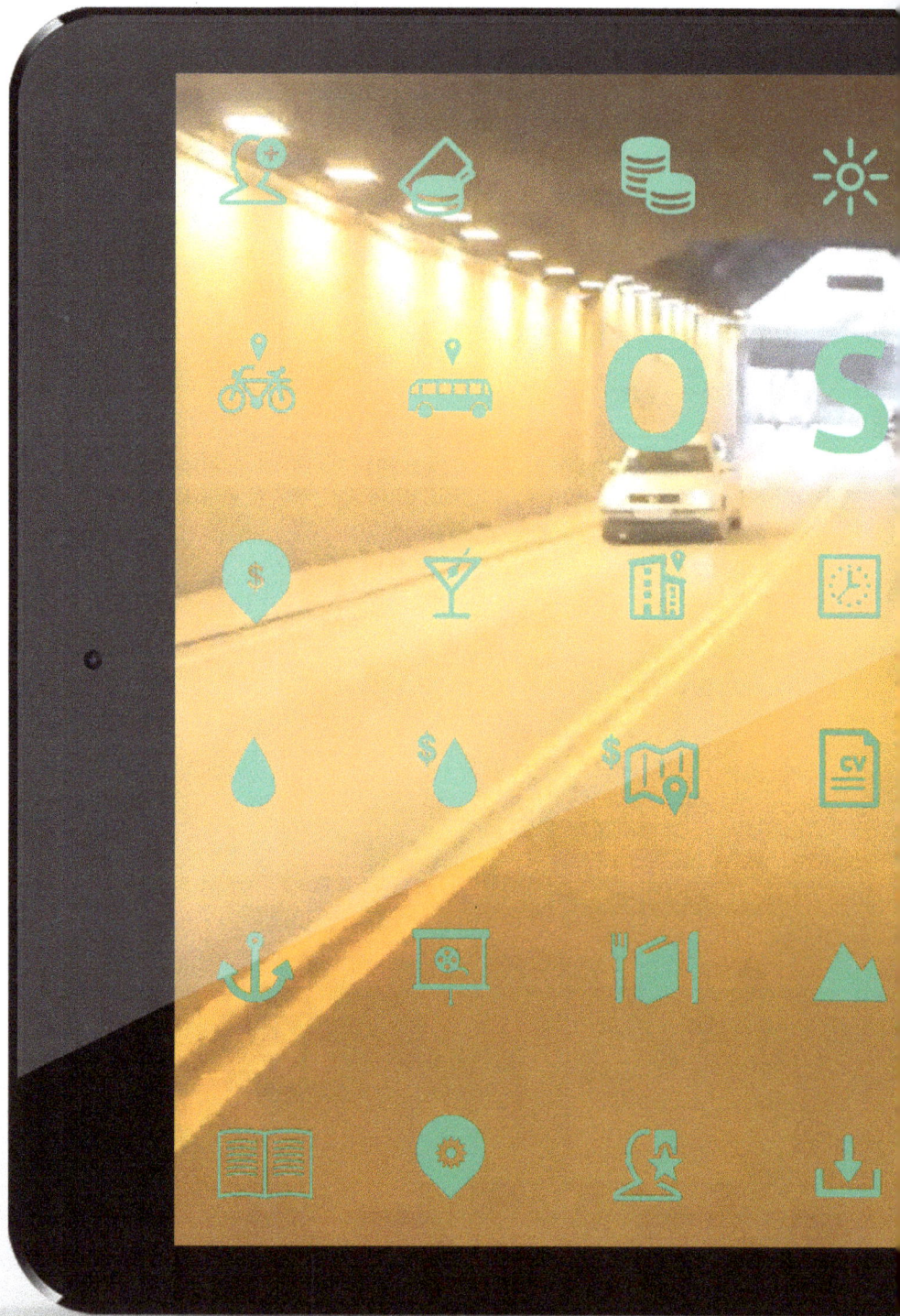

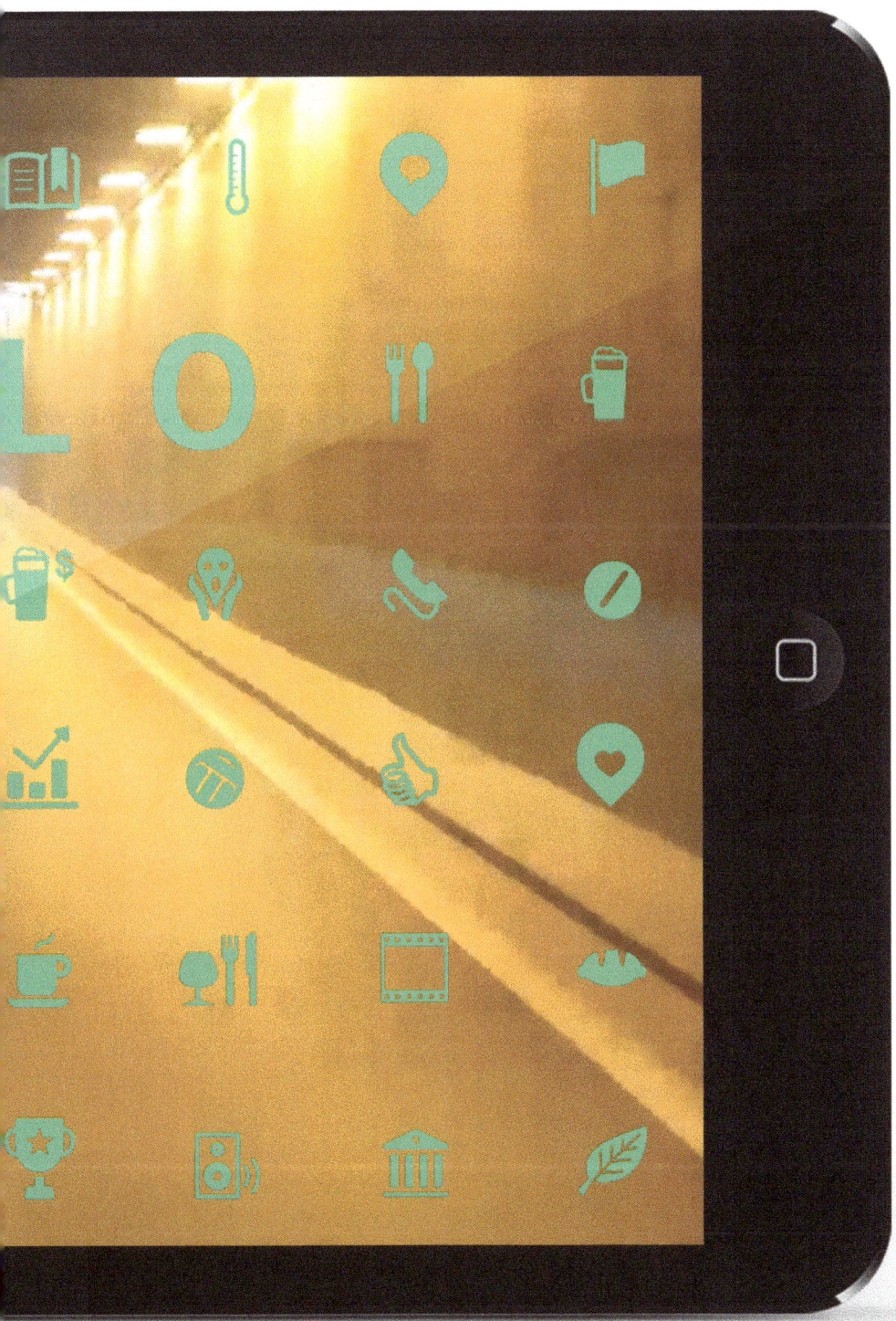

Have you ever felt like giving it up? Why didn't you?

Many times. But we did not give up because that is just not what we do. Also, the fact that we have pivoted the core of what Katachi Media does from a pure publishing house to a service provider helps keep the enthusiasm alive within the organization. But we've had to focus. We have bigger plans and ideas than we have budgets. Still, we are nowhere near giving up on our vision just yet.

What factors do you think contributes to the success of a magazine?

Commercial success is marketing. Another critical success is the ability to use interactive elements to elevate the content.

What might contribute to its failure?

Primarily marketing.

Are you currently profitable? How long did it take before your publication began to see a profit or how soon do you expect to see one?

No, we are not currently profitable. Katachi Media will now be our main source of income and we are planning on being profitable by mid 2015. While working on this, we keep on selling services, live very cheaply, and have kind friends and family. Start-up and entrepreneurial life is not glamorous but it will be worth it in the end! We truly believe that.

How do you go about setting a budget for the magazine?

We set the budget according to what we have available, which is not much, and then we have to work within that.

What are your major revenue streams right now? Which streams are you focused on developing?

We have changed most of our focus to licensing of the tool and are financing the development of the tool by performing services for clients. But our primary focus will change back to publishing in 2015 and we are really looking forward to that.

Tell me about your ad sales strategy? How did you go about getting advertisers?

We have had very little ad sales. We require our advertisers to create proper interactive ads, which when we started out, was not standard. We were usually provided with print material that we had to try and make something interesting out of. I believe this has changed a little since we started because some of those advertisers have matured.

What do you foresee for the digital magazine publishing industry in general?

I see magazines falling into two categories. One where it will basically be channel play. The digital version of the magazine will provide support for the parent print product and will primarily just be available for free. The other category will actually be paid for by readers and will provide an interactive experience that can't be paralleled either in print or on the web.

What kinds of skills do you think are vital for someone who is interested in becoming a digital magazine publisher?

I think you should have a lot of communication experience outside of print. The people making the most interesting things today are multi-disciplinary, curious people who want to tell good stories.

What last message of wisdom or inspiration would you like to leave with our readers who may be considering launching a digital publication themselves?

Since the medium also is the message, you need to ask yourself *why* your magazine should be in this medium. You need to have a very grounded understanding of where your decisions are coming from.

Is there anything else you'd like to add or you wish I had asked?

Yes, show respect for the medium—if what you are creating is virtually a print product, it should stay a print product. Now go make something amazing!

lionheart magazine

issue 4

Shapes

for the roar in your heart

seventy tree
helen bullock
NYC
the green kitchen
plate tectonics
oana befort

Lionheart Magazine 04

04

LionH

9

LIONHEART

HELEN MARTIN

Magazine name: *Lionheart*
Founder and editor: Helen Martin
Year founded: 2011
Tagline: For the roar in your heart
Editorial mission: A publication with wit, fun, and creativity
Location: Bristol, UK
Website: lionheart-mag.com
Formats: Print and blog
Issues per year: Two
Language: English
Reach: Selected countries worldwide.
Available: Website, digital newsstands, UK retail and department stores (Harrods, Selfridges, etc.)
Circulation: 2,000
Price per issue: £5 (approx. $7.50 USD)
One-year subscription: N/A
Size of in-house team: Two part-time

Lorraine: Helen, what did you do for a living before starting *Lionheart*?

Helen: I was a freelance writer. I did music editing and worked for a newspaper doing a bit of news reporting too. I also did court reporting and those kinds of things. I actually worked through the launch of my magazine and have continued to work ever since.

Has writing always been a passion of yours?

Yes, I've been telling and writing stories ever since I was very young, and ended up getting an English degree at a university in Cornwall. There I was lucky enough to meet loads of like-minded people. We'd sit around doing all the classic things like drinking wine, discussing our views on the world, and being oh so political. At the time we really thought we were amazing, but it was a really great place to gain a sense of confidence with regard to being creative. Although that was great, unfortunately I graduated right in the middle of a recession when there were no jobs at all, especially in the media field, so I ended up interning quite a bit and taking on a few odd jobs here and there.

How soon after college did the magazine come about? And why did you decide to launch one?

The magazine came about around three years later. After graduating from university I did my NCTJ, which is a journalism qualification, so as I said, I did some news reporting, reviewing, and I did a lot of pitching to local and national magazines as well. At the time I was trying to get as much experience as possible in the field. I later became the music editor for *Amelia's Magazine*. I really enjoyed that and gradually worked my way into the commissioning side of things. I also got to witness how valuable it was to build a network through social media.

One day, I was reading *frankie* magazine—which I absolutely love—and it dawned on me

that there was a huge gap in the UK market for something similar. Right there, I said to myself, "Fine. I'm going to do it. I'm going to start a magazine," and so I did [laughs].

Was there any market research or a business plan before you launched, or did you just go ahead and do it?

I conducted focus groups with people in London and from my local area. I gathered as many people as I could and tried to find out what they really wanted out of a new publication. It was really interesting as it turned out that a lot of people liked the Sunday supplement style of things, where they were intelligently spoken to, and of course, everybody just loved *frankie*. I actually pitched the magazine to some publishers, so I had to write a business plan as prior to that I was definitely just winging it.

Can you tell me what happened during that pitching process?

I had a few spreads that I showed. They were really into it but wanted me to compromise on things that I just wasn't willing to. They also wanted me to put a lot of money into it, while they would invest a minimal amount. I just thought to myself, "No, this isn't what it's about. It's supposed to be about this creation of a 'nice' magazine, not something that's overloaded with distracting ads everywhere," as they had wanted. So I ended up declining their offer and pitching to Waitrose instead, which is one of the big chain grocery stores here in the

UK. That process ended up really focusing me because it was then that the magazine became real in my mind. I was going up to people saying, "Hey, I've got this idea for a magazine. I've got a few spreads so you can get an idea of what it's about," and everyone I spoke to was so enthused about it. I also blogged the whole journey, but no, I didn't have any kind of stringent business plan.

So the plan that you wrote initially, was it more for the people you were pitching to or did it genuinely speak to you as well?

Yes, I did do it in my own little style. And as I said, it helped me focus and make the plan more succinct so it actually ended up being quite useful in the end.

Knowing what you know now, do you think it's important to create some type of plan before launching a magazine?

Yeah, yeah, I think so. I am definitely not that business-minded at all, I wish I was, but I go on this faith that people will like my magazine; so I'm on a mission to just get it out there.

How did you end up naming your magazine *Lionheart*?

That actually came back from one of the focus groups I held. I was talking with Jess Furseth, who's now one of my contributors, and we were discussing the topic of being passionate about something and having that fighting spirit, and she said, "Aah…lionheart…that's what that means."

And that was it? *Lionheart* **just stuck with you from there?**

Yeah. I thought *Lionheart Magazine* sounded pretty cool, but it's really hard to think of a name for a magazine.

I noticed that your first issue was entitled "Bravery." What made you pick that particular theme?

Because it was just so scary to launch the magazine—actually it was terrifying. There was so much I didn't know, especially on the business side of things, everything from distribution to getting the right paper stock to having a few ads if I could. I used to have sleepless nights over the possibility of a comma being in the wrong place [laughs]. But I feel that bravery really talks to people, as we all have to do things that can be scary at times.

How did you fund the very first issue of your magazine?

I used to write really long letters to my gran who lived in Ireland, and when she died she left me a little bit of money. It wasn't enough for a deposit on a house or anything like that but it was enough for me to potentially do a project that I'd really like to do, so I ended up putting some of it towards my magazine.

That's beautiful. What was your initial vision for the publication, has it changed any?

No, it's always stayed the same. It's just to create something that was friendly, fun, artsy, and intelligent. To have interviews that would

really get behind people. And also to create a place where writers and illustrators could feel free to do whatever they wanted, where we would all have the same vision for the magazine in a way that would allow readers to feel the energy and allow them to feel good about themselves also.

What makes *Lionheart Magazine* **different from other magazines out there that are in the same subject category?**

Yes, there's so much out there now. I have always appreciated all the other magazines, I think they're amazing. I've always kept the *Lionheart* ethos the same and kept its voice throughout, although I feel that it improves with every issue. I think it's like a journey that people are coming on, it's growing but it's not as potentially aspirational as some of the other titles out there, although it is aspirational in a good way, it's much more relaxed, easygoing, and subtle. It's just an all-round feel-good magazine really.

I see what you mean. What does your audience look like? Do they primarily look like you?

Yeah. Yeah, I guess so. Women in their twenties and thirties are probably the key demographic, but I also have lots of people in their forties and fifties as well. There are a lot of mums and older ladies who seem to enjoy the magazine, and then we have a load of students too.

How were you able to attract readers at the start? How did they find out about you?

rose
darling

Interview by *Sarah Ashworth*

_____ In the surf at dawn, creating patterns for Topshop by lunch. Designer and illustrator Rose Darling has Lionheart drawn all over her. And yes, that's her actual surname.

I'm told I notice things that others don't, like patterns on certain objects. My mum attended Chelsea School of Art earlier than most people and my sisters all drew; I was inspired. It was inevitable I would go into illustration.

I get fidgety easily and need to do as much as possible. After university I joined sports and lifestyle brand Animal, creating designs that ended up in their collections, or on sponsored riders' t-shirts and accessories. I learnt print techniques, fabrics and factories. I then landed a job as the main designer with organic children clothing company, Frugi. It was good to work with a small company because I could really get stuck in.

I was nicknamed Worzel Gummidge because I'd jump straight out of the surf and come to work. People didn't understand the Cornish style. It's different in the city, there are so many alternative people that identify themselves through fashion. Designing for a fashion forecaster felt like walking into a fashion blog, it was like fancy dress every day of the week. I was surrounded by 6ft model-esque girls who wore hot pants to important meetings. It was different!

I'm drawn to Salvador Dali, illustrator Amy Brown and graffiti artist Kelsey Brookes. But working in trend forecasting you get inspired by different things at different times. Fashion works a few seasons ahead. When you're coming at design with a fresh pair of eyes its often extreme and unfamiliar. My job is translating it into something more popular.

The toughest design brief I had was to design men's socks. It was all comical or really basic designs. I found myself walking into shops and staring at the men's sock rails. I just couldn't get my head into being a man. The job ended up being passed onto a male designer.

Designing patterns is quite challenging. There are rules you can stick to such as half drops, but other times the spontaneity of designing a random pattern produces a much more exciting outcome.

At the moment I'm researching 60s sci-fi heroine characters, Barbarella, and lots of fancy dress for a belt-come-bodice piece of underwear. The best thing is that my work is so varied, one day I

Continues...

I blogged everything from meeting the bank manager to launching the magazine and beyond. I definitely would not have been able to launch this magazine without the use of social media. My blog caught on quite a bit, to the point where other people started blogging about the magazine and my journey as well.

How exactly do you use social media to reach your audience—connect with them, talk to them, and so forth?
Just completely like how I would talk to any of my friends.

So you're very real with your audience then?
Definitely. I think it's important to have a genuine person behind any sort of brand. I am definitely not going to put out anything pretentious. I wouldn't even know how to do that really [laughs].

Is there a certain "braveness" in being able to honestly have your voice out there? I'm probably the next generation up from you and we're a little bit more private and guarded. So I am wondering, is that something that's natural and easy for your generation, to just honestly put your thoughts and feelings out there, or is it something that you had to work on doing and build up the confidence for?
I definitely had to work on it. For example, I remember with the first blog post I ever wrote, I felt extremely exposed, I felt exposed writing about anything, actually. I think the generations after me are the ones who really go for it.

They're just out there like, "This is who I am," but I'm like, "Whoa, it's too much." It's quite scary, but we all write a lot about our feelings and things that we're going through. Funny enough, I don't necessarily like it when my family or close friends read my blog, I enjoy the anonymity of writing online.

What can you tell me about distribution? When you created that first issue, had you already been to Waitrose by then?
Yes, I had spoken to Waitrose and they had advised me to get a distributor who could act as the go-between, and that opened up a whole world of lessons for me with regard to learning about distribution.

So you began to learn about distribution prior to launching your first issue?
Yes. But although Waitrose was really keen, I mainly ended up distributing that first issue by myself. I did loads and loads of posting online which resulted in a lot of online sales and I also put them into all the shops myself. Comag, the distributor, eventually heard about the magazine, got ahold of me, and ended up taking over a big section of the distribution for me.

What were the number of copies you printed for your first print run?
Two thousand copies.

And you were literally just ringing up stores and being the salesperson for your magazine?
Yes, exactly.

What types of stores were you calling? Did you have a specific idea of where you wanted your magazine placed?

Yes, independent bookshops, stationery shops, and small boutiques. I wanted everything to have somewhat of an independent feel to it. Even though I had been to Waitrose, I kind of did that on a whim and never really expected them to actually email me back. So I went to small, cutesy-type shops and places where I could go and have a chat with the people behind the counter. I wanted my little distribution system to be almost as personal as the magazine. I also knew that they would talk about the mag in a nice way and create a nice little social communities online. But once Comag got involved, they were really good at getting it into a lot of the stores around London.

So Comag came to you—is this after issue one or issue two?

Well, issue one had been out for four months and one day I sent a speculative email to them and to my surprise they contacted me right back. The gentleman who responded offered to drive out and see me; so we set up a meeting and he told me that he distributed *frankie* and *Lula* magazines and could see my publication in line with those.

And they distribute worldwide?

Yes. I know that *Lionheart* is in some cool shops in Canada and Singapore and some other places, so yes it is worldwide but not on a mega scale yet.

As far as the magazine goes, how many people do you have working in-house? Is it just you?

There are two of us. My designer Dan Bright, who also lives in Bristol, and me. We used to work together and it was literally on our lunch breaks that we would go work on *Lionheart* and then after work we'd go to the pub and work on it some more—it was like an addiction…a good addiction though [laughs]. The last few issues have also had Holly Giblin designing a selection of the features—like Dan, she adds wonderful illustrations to pieces and puts so much thought into everything she does.

Being out twice a year does it typically take about six months to put together an issue?

No, we probably do it in the last two to three months before a release is due. Ideas brew for months and months though. When we put out an issue we're usually like, "Hmm, should we do that again?" [laughs].

Can you give me an idea of how you plan things out, from the TOC to the final layout?

It's basically millions and millions of scrapbooks of loads of ideas that I throw around and then I organize them somehow and commission them out.

Are these your own personal scrapbooks or are you looking at others' online?

My own. I have scrapbooks full of torn pieces of paper and I also have little ones, kind of like little Pinterest boards. I've also got notebooks that are full of everything you can imagine.

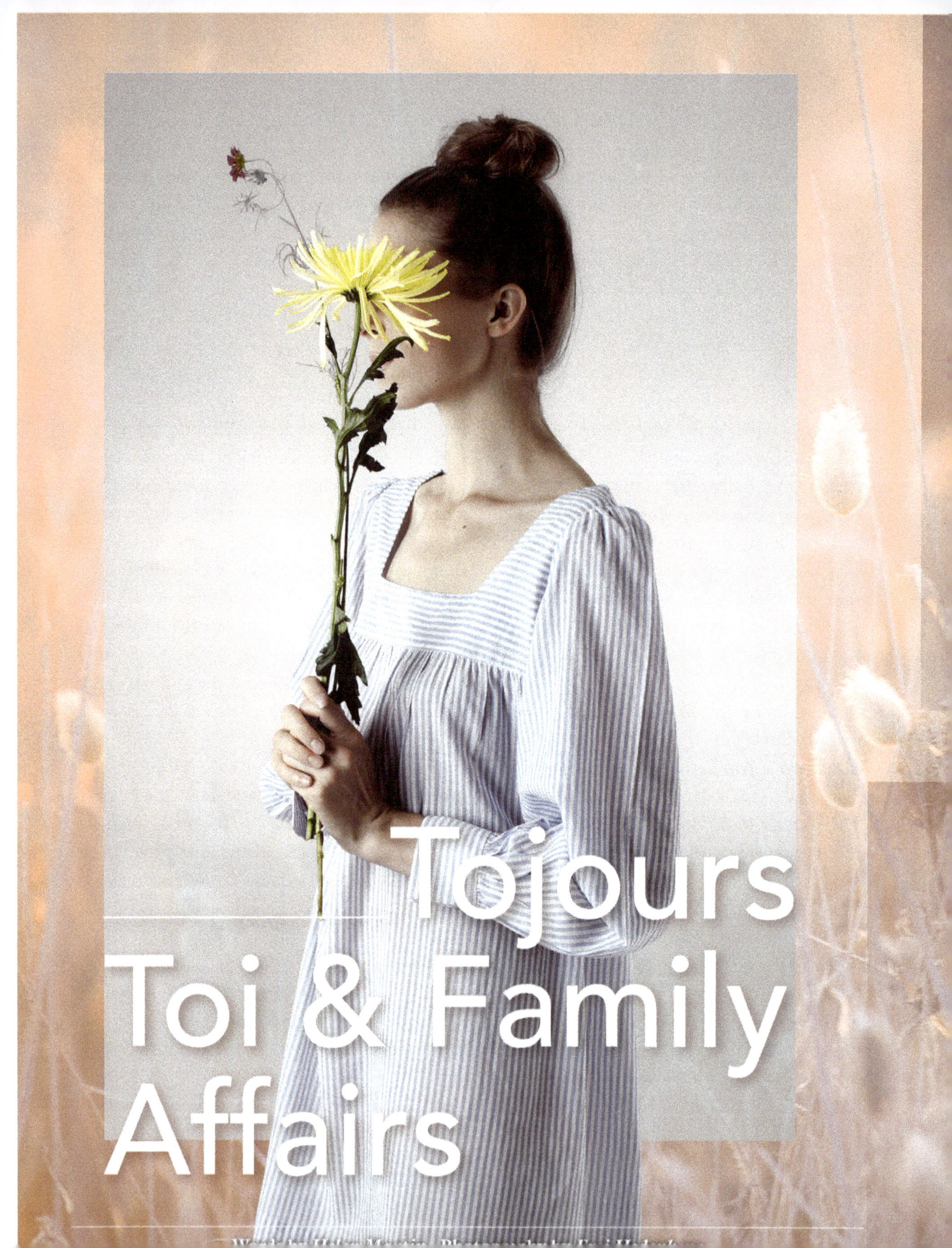

Tojours Toi & Family Affairs

Nina sends packages tied with string, full of visual inspiration: fabrics, colours and shapes sail across the merry seas. Then together they delve into Kaya's archives and pull designs, which they adjust and refine to create the shape and detail for each piece.

The Family Affair: Nina and Kaya Egli are a mother and daughter partnership, together forming Family Affairs. Kaya – based in Switzerland – first opened her own store at the age of 20, going on to become the in-house designer for The Beatles Apple shop, in London. Nina – based in New York has her own line of jewellery. Toujours Toi

Then I say, "This is what I should be doing—oh no—what about this and this?" Eventually I organize all the ideas and start talking to contributors and commissioning the pieces out. I'll tell the writers what the theme is and we'll go back and forth in a kind of creative process. We'll talk about the illustrations that might go along with the idea and talk to the designer to see how many pages we think the story can go across. It's not as organized as it should be, but I just think that's part of the job. My designer and I work really well together and there's not that much back and forth between us because we are both pretty much on the same page. Finally, when it all comes together we spend ages just double-checking and looking through.

Do you have a regular set of contributors?
Yes I do. I have my key ones—who are absolutely fantastic and I feel very lucky indeed to have them onboard—but of course I am always on the lookout for others as well.

About how many regulars do you have?
Probably about ten.

Who does the illustrations on the covers? They're absolutely beautiful.
I've had the covers illustrated by different people—Gemma Milly, Holly Exley, Natasha Thompson, and Faye West.

I would never have guessed that different people illustrated the covers because they all just have this certain style and feel to them.

They do, but it's interesting because it's quite different to have an illustration on the cover of a magazine. I thought about changing it and putting something like a wallpaper pattern or a photo on the cover, but I think there is something really powerful about those images on the stands so I'm going to stick with it. Plus people have been really positive about them too.

So the feedback's been good?
Really good. I think illustration is so amazing and such a talent—the impact is really cool. I think the last one looks great, but I always think the latest issue is obviously the best, because you have to really.

[Laughs] And it probably *is* getting better with each issue. Tell me, what's the most challenging part of running a magazine? You may have already touched on it a little earlier.
Yes, I would say the business and all the admin that I just didn't necessarily expect, because after all, it's just me. All the mailing out, sorting out the distribution, dealing with the invoices, trying to get the ads in, just basically all the bits and pieces that go along with running a magazine, it's so time consuming. Then you're running the social media, working on the website, blogging. It's really a lot!

And you don't have help with any of those duties yet?
I probably should be delegating a lot of that out, but that is one of my weaknesses—I am always saying "Oh, it's fine. Don't worry about it."

issue 3

lionheart magazine

for the roar in your heart

adventure

lanterns on the lake
flowers
london
first love
the adventurists
jam
yurt life
anorak

Lion Heart Magazine

£5

9 772049 696001 03

Believe me, I know what you mean. Okay, so what's the most rewarding part of creating the magazine for you?

I love seeing it when it first comes out and it looks amazing. I love the emails I get from people that really enjoy it and all the Facebook posts and those types of things. The fact that people get something out of it and have been inspired, or they just felt good from reading it—which is exactly what the purpose was in the first place—is extremely rewarding.

What factors contribute to the success of a magazine, do you think?

Business [laughs]. I think having your ethos and sticking with it, and if you are changing slightly don't forget to take your readers along with you. Always treat your readers with respect. They are amazing, they love you, and they love your brand. They are like your friends, so be kind. For success in general though, if you can get some good, solid business advice, then definitely do that.

What do you think can ultimately contribute to a magazine's failure?

I think losing the vision that you had can do it. If you lose the passion I think people can tell, but it's a really hard industry. To make money from it is hard and, yeah, it's tricky, but I am hoping that *Lionheart* just continues to go on, so I almost refuse to look at failure really.

Are you currently profitable?

By the tiniest amount.

That's great. Do you set some a budget for each issue of the magazine?

I do. Basically, I have a set amount that I make back from the magazine and then I just say that's what I've got and that's all I can afford to spend. But I'd love to be able to pay people properly one day.

So you base it upon what you make and then that is obviously what you can spend?

Yes. Plus some of it has to go towards the website, some of it needs to go to renewing the fees, and things like that. So there's not a very big budget, if any budget at all.

Luckily people are like, "I believe in *Lionheart*, and I want to see it grow," so they continue to work for it, improving it every time. I've never been a fan of having them work for free, having done it so many times myself, but I think that's a classic issue with running an independent magazine.

Are your major revenue streams from advertising, subscriptions, or single-issue sales?

Single-issue sales.

What are you focused on growing, the sales or the advertising, or just everything?

I've reached a point now where I need to focus more on the business side of things, but my number one will always be the single sales because they're the people we're making the magazine for who and hopefully will continue to keep loving it.

How do you pick your advertisers then? Do you look at products you would personally use and think your audience might use? Do you pick them or do they pick you—how does that work?

In the past they've contacted me mostly. I've had an art gallery and those types of advertisers, but it has to be people that fit in with the brand. We don't have very much advertising at the moment, it's only like a few pages but we hope to grow that in time.

I also have spots that I give people who own independent small businesses, so they can have a sixth of a page or something like that for a reasonable fee. It's been more of a grass-rootsy type thing to support them, but obviously bigger companies and brands will need to pay more.

What types of skills do you think are important for magazine publishers to have today?

Organization skills definitely. A good grasp of social media because the people that you connect with online are going to help you through in some way. And then, of course you have to have a massive load of creativity too.

Is there a last message of wisdom or inspiration that you would like to leave with someone who may be thinking of starting their own publication?

I would say definitely, 100 percent, go for it. Put everything into it. Don't underestimate the amount of work that's going to be involved but you will absolutely love it. It will all be worth it in the end.

9 771745 916048

Issue 55   Sep/Oct '14   £6

Little White Lies

Truth & Movies

Maps to the Stars

LITTLE WHITE LIES

DAVID JENKINS

Magazine name: *Little White Lies*
Editor: David Jenkins
Year founded: 2005
Tagline: Truth and movies
Editorial mission: To talk about movies with passion and honesty
Location: London, UK
Website: littlewhitelies.co.uk
Formats: Print, blog, and digital
Issues per year: Six
Language: English
Reach: Worldwide
Available: Website, digital newsstands, and select newsstands
Circulation: 45,000
Price per issue: £6 (approx. $9 USD)
One-year subscription: £29 (approx. $44 USD)
Size of in-house team: Twenty-four full-time

Lorraine: David, what were you doing before you launched *Little White Lies*?

David: Well, I didn't actually launch the mag, but I've been on board since before the first issue came out. I am primarily a journalist and did a postgraduate diploma in magazine journalism at City University. The guys who were setting up the magazine sent an email to our course instructor looking for people who'd be interested in contributing to the first issue. At the time I hadn't really decided on the direction I wanted to go in yet, so when that email arrived I felt that it was something that I could focus on and so got in touch right away and started freelancing for them. Their first editions were mostly created with work from free contributions as it was one of those things where one person just couldn't write it all; so for the sake of diversity and giving some young writers a byline and a print pedestal for their career, they took a few of us on board—I thought it was a great opportunity.

How did you manage to go from opportunity to editor?

Well, after doing all this free stuff for *Little White Lies* I let them know that I thought the magazine was great and that I was quite happy to continue working on it, building up my portfolio with them. Eventually I became a section editor but continued to freelance doing bits and bobs and writing one-off pieces for other magazines and newspapers. I then did an extended internship at *Time Out London* and wound up landing a full-time job on the film section there. Although I was getting a salary from *Time Out*, I always kept in close contact with the guys at *Little White Lies*, helping out wherever I could—sometimes even writing for them under a pseudonym.

While I was still at *Time Out*, *Little White Lies* continued to expand to the point where they had salaried staff and were doing other things beyond the print iteration, so they offered me

a place as the reviews editor. I took the job for about a year and then the editor moved on, so I ended up stepping into the role.

Were movies always a passion of yours or did you just happen to get into it because it was the first opportunity you received while you were at college?

I guess I like movies as much as most people, maybe a little more than the average cinema-goer. I had watched a lot of indie and foreign films in my junior year at university but had never really written about them. I didn't study film at university so I've never had any formal training in writing about films, but as soon as I made that decision to get into the world of film I just knew I'd have to totally immerse myself in the subject.

I see.

I mean you read a lot of other critics and writers and you immediately understand that their depth of knowledge is just huge, so if you're going to be competing with them—competing is the wrong word—but if you're going to have work published alongside them as part of a wider cultural conversation then you really have to know your stuff, know your onions so to speak [laughs].

Where did the name *Little White Lies* come from?

It's a bit of a weird one; it's actually a lyric from a popular Radiohead song called "Motion Picture Soundtrack."

Now that makes sense.

Yes, Danny Miller created the magazine while doing a design illustration course at university and made *Little White Lies*: Issue 0 as his final project. He is a massive Radiohead fan.

What was the initial vision for the magazine?

The magazine originally started out with the concept that movies don't exist inside a bubble, they are about the real world and reflect the real world, and it shouldn't just be this very hermetic cultural conversation. The idea for *Little White Lies* was to latch onto a concept in a film and talk about that concept even if it wasn't explicitly about the movie itself. For instance, if we put a sci-fi movie on the cover there would be scope to talk about interstellar travel, spaceships, and the realities of space. There's this sort of digressive nature to it all as we discuss ideas that are formed by the movie, but not necessarily about the movie. From the time I became editor I slightly changed what the magazine is about and its intentions as a magazine. It's not that I thought the original idea was not good or not working but it was because I didn't feel that it really reflected my knowledge and skills, since my expertise is movies.

How are you able to stand out from the competition that's covering the same territory, whether their format is print, blog, or digital? How do you manage to keep publishing as successfully as you are?

Well, it's a toughie. Not talking about the competition for a moment, I think how we've managed to keep publishing is because the magazine itself is like a house, it's the thing that people see, but then we have all these other things we do like our social networks, our website, an app for phones, and all these other things that are like the foundations that keeps the house up—where one couldn't exist without the other. Maybe there was a point, when we first started out ten years ago, where a magazine could exist and make money through print advertising alone, but when the economic crash happened—as I'm sure you must have heard from other publishers—the bottom fell out from under that model.

My feeling is that a lot of the advertisers started to need the tangibility that you can get online, where you can actually see the numbers of people who are looking at or clicking on your content, and because of that you are able to judge popularity in a very definite way. But with a magazine they almost just have to take the magazine's word for it that their message is going to reach a certain audience and a certain number of readers.

In terms of the movie magazine space, I love reading other magazines. I love *Sight and Sound*, for instance. But I don't read other mags and think, "I like that, I like that, and we can do something similar." I read them for my enjoyment, not as a way to find out or deduce our place in the market. I think that you don't really need to strive to do something pointedly different from someone else, it's more that you just try to do good, interesting work—something that a reader is going to enjoy. With *Little White Lies* although our written content might have a bit of overlap with other magazines, it's the way that it's presented and the fact that it's illustrated are what makes it different.

Who is the magazine aimed at? What does your audience look like?

Ah, that's a good question. I think it's good to have that element of uncertainty because it keeps you thinking and you can be open to surprises of what kind of people *might* pick the magazine up and what kind of people *could* pick it up. If you reach that point where you're just creating things for a specific set of people then I feel that it becomes exclusive and niche and I think you lose that sense of trying to reach the broadest audience possible.

That's a great answer as it definitely presents a different perspective on the matter.

I will say, however, that younger people tend to buy the magazine and lots of people who are into design buy the magazine, but I wouldn't necessarily say that that's our core audience.

What about attracting readers online and offline? You've mentioned having an app, social media presence, as well as a website that all run alongside the magazine, but how do you coordinate them all to work together? Can they be coordinated? Is it somewhat of a cohesive effort or do you view each channel as a totally separate entity?

NORTH CARTHAGE POLICE DEPT. 18 NCPD 55 — STATE OF — MISSOURI

MISSING PERSONS

RESTRICTED CASE FILE

CONFIDENTIAL

LWL 1808201¼
PAGE NUMBER
1 OF 8   047

DAVID FINCHER
DETECTIVE
MISSING PERSONS

Q LW (ES):
It's an interesting role for Ben Affleck to play. I felt there was a lot of crossover with his character in Terrence Malick's To The Wonder.

A FINCHER:
Hmm. Maybe. I've seen To The Wonder and... it's different, but related. Yeah, it's funny because I was walking off the sound stage one day and I overheard Rosamund [Pike] talking to Ren. She was saying, "what do you think David saw in my work that made him think of casting me for this role?" Ren said, "I dunno, I couldn't tell you." I walked over and said, "The question you should be asking is, what have I seen in Ren's work that made me cast him." He laughed. ████ But it is. It's not the kind of role that most leading men go looking for. Yes, I'd like for someone to take a steamroller and grind me in to paste veeery slowly.

Q LW (ES):
Are you looking at other movies when casting?

A FINCHER:
Yes, but I'm also looking at "the person". I hadn't seen all of Rosamund's work. I'd seen four or five things. The Bond movie, Jack Reacher. They always seemed to be two years apart. I was intrigued that, even after seeing four of five movies, I had no sense of her. She was sort-of opaque. In An Education, I even found myself not being aware of what her age was. That was an intriguing thing. Then I met her and she had the most important thing that Amy needed to have, which is that Rosamund was raised as an only child. You just feel it. It's not that she's not socialized, but that she's an orchid. She has that sense. It's not entitlement, but if you've spent your young life being around adults and not other kids, you carry yourself differently. Ren's thing was that he has lived through this kind of "attention". You can tell that he has made his peace with it. He has considerable charm. You can tell that's he's willing to trade on that. Oftentimes, that can lead to sticky things becoming stickier. ████ And that was key — you have to have that to be Nick. He's really bright as an actor. He was willing to demean himself.

Q LW (ES):
In past interviews I've often read you talking about "putting the camera where it should be."

A FINCHER:
By that I mean, where you think the story is. The most fun part of executive producing a TV show [House of Cards] was seeing everyone else's dailies. It's so weird because you've read the script, you've seen storyboards, if it's a complicated sequence, you've listened to the read-through. Then the dailies come in and you're like, "Really?! That side of the Oval Office is where you think that scene is?!" It was interesting seeing stuff filter in. Stuff I would've never thought would be a quiet moment or a tossed-off moment at the end of the scene. A lot of cases, I'd be thinking why are we here, why are we looking at this thing in this way, and as the coverage progressed, you see what's going on. He's making the most out of this or that. Sometimes you have to wait for people to show you their hand and what they're capable of and what they're thinking. I feel that in this business you bet on horses not races. The greatest thing about doing House of Cards was telling all these directors that they have final cut. I'm gonna shine in, but I definitely know how to go fuck myself. If you give people that authority and respect, they're going to work harder. It was an interesting lesson. I know that for me it's really important to get the master just right. I'm a little more didactic about that first communication of an idea.

Q LW (ES):
Did the process of working in TV change how you worked on Gone Girl?

A FINCHER:
No. I don't think so. On House of Cards, we were told that we had to work fast a we couldn't shoot 20 takes. And I did it anyway. It's the only way I know how. The first three are rehearsals. Then you start making 11 more concise, weeding out the bad stuff. I don't think I moved any faster. I took 100 days to shoot this movie. I think for me, House of Cards was fun for me having that company, all those faces, to go in and work with every day. Making Gone Girl, I was probably more attuned to finding a good ensemble. ████ I was more interested in doing something with a group of eight or ten really good actors as opposed to doing something with two or three. I ████ enjoy the rehearsal part. Figuring out the tone.

Q LW (ES):
Is it hard for you to say, this is the final movie, this is where we stop? Could you go on forever?

A FINCHER:
No. One could, but I don't think I could. There will always be scenes which you think could be better. The weird thing is that, for the most part, the scenes you look at and think are going to be really hard, those are the scenes you spend all the time and money orchestrating. Then there's always some little stupid scene that should go off without a hitch that you have to go back and reshoot 11 two, three times. Then you cut it. The hanging chaos of movies.

Q LW (ES):
Do you have a better idea of what those hanging chads will ████ be now than you did, say, ten years ago?

A FINCHER:
No. They're always a surprise, because if they weren't you'd be planning for them. It's always like, how are we going to age a guy in reverse? That's what all the money gets spent on. That part was easy. Where we left with, how you gonna work with 84-year-old extras? Oh my... I forget, that's going to be really hard. You never quite get it all the way you'd wanna.

Q LW (ES):
Is filmmaking replicating an image you already ████ have in your head?

A FINCHER:
No, no. Maybe it was initially, when you're first trying to facilitate a shooting schedule or be involved in movies, or commercials. All you know to look at is what you saw. As you get more comfortable, you realize that when you're shooting and you've done 15 takes or something, they don't have to be a refinement of the same idea. Often, we see directors working and we think that they're taking something and they're minutely tightening it. There are also times when you have to pull the pin and let the pressure off. So you say, now do a take like you've never met. Just as a palate cleanser. I think you should have a very specific idea of what it is that you want. All of us together trying to catch lighting in a bottle on a given day.

Q LW (ES):
Is modulation of an image more than a refinement?

A FINCHER:
I'd say, you've written the music, all the orchestra's there. But to only do what was written is maybe not to take advantage of a great first violin, or a great oboe player. There are times when you just want people to deliver information, and there are times when you want a solo.

Q LW (ES):
I'm naive about the physical process of making movies.

A FINCHER:
Really?

Q LW (ES):
I don't think I've experienced that side of things in any meaningful way.

A FINCHER:
You have to. You have to if you're going to write about film. The imperfection of it and the grab-ass problem solving doucebaggery of it is incredibly important in understanding what goes on. The movie business did this to itself. The reason why the movie business is so expensive is there's this perception that everything is done perfectly. There's this belief in infrastructure and training and the fact that everyone is so specialised. I remember, especially when I was at Industrial Light and Magic, I was 19, the whole idea that what George Lucas had built this new NASA, this incredibly efficient system. And it wasn't.

> **"NINETY PEOPLE WORKING TOGETHER CANNOT FIND THEIR ASS WITH A FLASHLIGHT."**

You have to realize how much luck goes into making a movie. For the most part, we don't get in test movies any more, thanks to previews crashers. So it's incredibly important if you're writing about film to see how it gets made. Not to say that to write about sausage you need to see sausage being made, but I do think there's this fucked up perception that everything is measured in advance and everyone knows what the outcome's gonna be. That's just not the case. It's much more like tennis. You can win or lose a match based on a couple of nerves or a couple of returns you miss, and in the same way, you can fuck a whole scene up.

A lot of what you're doing as a director is mitigating against a disastrous outcome. It's an interesting time to make movies, though. Talking about specialisation — the reason movies have gotten more expensive is because the perception is that everything we're doing is very, very precious and has to be done perfectly. It's not like you go and rent a car and the character drives a car. You have to rent a fleet of them in case one breaks. It's a perceived importance. There's this sense that it's a military operation. And it is a military operation, and if you've never seen a military operation you'd be shocked that anyone ever comes out alive. Ninety people working together cannot find their ass with a flashlight.

Q LW (ES):
Did you see Soderbergh's speech in San Francisco? He was lamenting the death of medium-sized movies.

A FINCHER:
They're too risky. If you look at movies like... I guess, All The President's Men was important enough and based on a big enough transgression, but take a movie like Klute — I don't think that movie would be made today. I mean, The Godfather would have a hard time being made today. Even if you could put up the $75 million it would take to make that movie today, and you could guarantee that it would be one of the greatest movies of all time, people would still go. $75 million? I dunno man, that's a lot of bread — There are realities to our business. The bottom has fallen out. Drama that cost more than $30 million, you're taking a big risk. I think Soderbergh was right. And it's sad. I think the thing is to make movies cheaper. People are migrating to television to find characters that aren't spandex-clad superheroes.

Q LW (ES):
Have you ever had one of these mega blockbusters dangled in front of you?

A FINCHER:
I don't think anyone would come to me with a money-is-no-object proposition. No, I was ready to go to Australia and make 20,000 Leagues Under the Sea, which was going to be a big tentpole summer movie, but there was a lot of riptide to it. It was not just the hero's journey.

Q LW (ES):
Was it a case of, as they say, creative differences?

A FINCHER:
I don't think culture and corporate anxieties. Once we got past the list of people we could cast as the different characters in the film, once we got past one or two names which made them very comfortable, making a movie at that price, it became this bizarre endeavor to find which three names you could rub together to make platinum.

Page 3

CASE NO. **LWL0066**

MISSING PERSONS UNIT
NORTH CARTHAGE POLICE DEPT. MISSOURI.

INVESTIGATIVE REPO(RT)

CASE STATUS:

MISSING

INVESTIGATION WITH: DAVID FINCHER - DIRECTOR OF *GONE GIRL*
DEPARTMENT: LITTLE WHITE LIES MAGAZINE
INVESTIGATING OFFICER: DAVID JENKINS - EDITOR   I.D. NO. 00022800
SKETCH ARTIST: TIMBA SMITS - CREATIVE DIRECTOR

MISSING PERSON/S: FULL NAME: MRS. AMY DUNNE
ADDRESS: NO.7 MCMANSION DRIVE, NORTH CARTHAGE
SUBURB/TOWN/CITY: MISSOURI   ZIP CODE: 1401200

CASE SYNOPSIS:
THE SUBJECT WAS REPORTED AS MISSING ON THE DAY OF HER FIFTH WEDDING ANNIVERSARY - JUNE, '15 2012. MARRIED TO NICHOLAS DUNNE (SEE ATTACHED INVESTIGATIVE REPORT) - NCPD'S LEAD SUSPECT IN HER DISSAPEARANCE.

AHEAD OF HIS HIGHLY ANTICIPATED ADAPTATION OF GILLIAN FLYNN'S PSYCHOLOGICAL BEST-SELLER, *GONE GIRL*, LWLIES IS GRANTED AN AUDIENCE WITH DIRECTOR DAVID FINCHER.

- DETAILS OF INVESTIGATION -

DAVID FINCHER IS A DIRECTOR WHO REQUIRES NO REAL INTRODUCTION. HE'S THOUGHT OF AS A SAVIOUR OF AMERICAN NEO-NOIR WITH THE FASTIDIOUSNESS OF KUBRICK. WITH TITLES LIKE *SEVEN*, *ZODIAC*, *THE SOCIAL NETWORK* AND *THE CURIOUS CASE OF BENJAMIN BUTTON* TO HIS NAME, HE'S CREATED SOME OF THE MOST MEMORABLE AND INNOVATIVE - AND NOT TO MENTION, GREATEST - FILMS OF THE LATE TWENTIETH AND EARLY TWENTYFIRST CENTURY. FOR HIS LATEST ENDEAVOUR, HE HAS TAKEN ON ACMOTHER? LITERARY BEHEMOTH (FOLLOWING HIS TAKE ON STIEG LARSSON'S *THE GIRL WITH THE DRAGON TATTOO*), THIS TIME IS GILLIAN FLYNN BRUTAL, PERSPECTIVE-SWITCHING KIDNAP SAGA, *GONE GIRL*. HERE, HE TALKS ABOUT THE CHALLENGES OF BRINGING THIS FILM TO THE SCREEN, BUT ALSO ON CRUDE PUBLIC PERCEPTIONS OF HOLLYWOOD AND MOVIEMAKING.

INTERVIEW WITH DAVID FINCHER:

[Interview text partially redacted]

APPROVAL AND REVIEW
SIGNED:
INVESTIGATING OFFICER: DAVID JENKINS - EDITOR
ID NUMBER: 00022800
LOCATION OF REPORT/STATEMENT: NORTH CARTHAGE P.B. MISSOURI
STATUS: COPY
LWL 18082014
PAGE NUMBER 3 OF 8   049

3

Page 4

STANDARD CONTINUATION PAGE

FOR INVESTIGATION OF: DAVID FINCHER - DIRECTOR OF *GONE GIRL*
REPORT DATE: MONDAY 18 AUGUST, 2014
FILED: ☐ Y ☐ N

[Interview Q&A text, much redacted]

> "THERE'S DEFINITELY A *RASHOMON* SENSE OF HOW THINGS ARE REMEMBERED BY CERTAIN CHARACTERS."

READ ONLY REPORT
INVESTIGATING OFFICER: DAVID JENKINS - EDITOR
DEPARTMENT: MISSING PERSONS
ID NUMBER: 00022800
LOCATION OF REPORT/STATEMENT: NORTH CARTHAGE P.B. MISSOURI
STATUS: COPY
LWL 18082014
PAGE NUMBER 4 OF 8   050

4

Page 7

INTERVIEW WITH: DAVID FINCHER - DIRECTOR OF *GONE GIRL*
CASE NO. **LWL0066**

MISSING PERSONS UNIT
NORTH CARTHAGE POLICE DEPT. MISSOURI.

INVESTIGATIVE REPO(RT)

CASE STATUS:

SUSPECT

DEPARTMENT: LITTLE WHITE LIES MAGAZINE
INVESTIGATING OFFICER: DAVID JENKINS - EDITOR   I.D. NO. 00022800
DEPT: MISSING PERSONS UNIT
LOCATION WHERE STATEMENT WAS TAKEN: NORTH CARTHAGE PD, MISSOURI

ACCUSED PERSON: ☐ M ☐ F   FULL NAME: MR. NICK DUNNE
ADDRESS: NO.7 MCMANSION DRIVE, NORTH CARTHAGE
SUBURB/TOWN/CITY: MISSOURI   ZIP CODE: 1401200

FINGERPRINTS:
LEFT THUMB   RIGHT THUMB   INDEX FINGERS

NCPD
DUNNE, MR
DOB AUG 15 1978   MALE

- DETAILS OF INVESTIGATION -

> "IT'S FASCINATING TO ME THAT CONTENT ALMOST MEANS THE OPPOSITE OF WHAT IT'S INTENDED TO MEAN."

[Interview Q&A text, partially redacted]

>>> *GONE GIRL* IS RELEASED IN CINEMAS ON OCTOBER 3, 2014.

APPROVAL AND REVIEW
SIGNED:
INVESTIGATING OFFICER: DAVID JENKINS - EDITOR
ID NUMBER: 00022800
LOCATION OF REPORT/STATEMENT: NORTH CARTHAGE P.B. MISSOURI
STATUS: COPY
LWL 18082014
PAGE NUMBER 7 OF 8   053

7

Page 8

MISSING PERSONS UNIT
NORTH CARTHAGE POLICE DEPT. MISSOURI.

RECORDS ADMINISTRATION BRANCH

MATERIAL MUST NOT BE REMOVED NOR ADDED TO THIS FILE

WITHOUT APPROVAL OF THE RECORDS ADMINISTRATION BRANCH

By order of the Attorney General

THIS FILE HAS BEEN CHARGED AS INDICATED BELOW

TO TRANSFER – Notify the Missing Persons Unit, NCPD, Missouri

Requested by	Division	Date Issued	Recorded
DET. S M KAUFMAN	LWLIES EDIT DEPT.	02.10.2013	☐ Y ☐ N
SGT. O STAFFORD	DESIGN DEPT.	19.08.2014	☐ Y ☐ N
SGT. L BOGLIO	DESIGN DEPT.	19.08.2014	☐ Y ☐ N
DET. A WOODWARD	LWLIES EDIT DEPT.	19.08.2014	☐ Y ☐ N
DET. T SMITS	CREATIVE DEPT.	20.08.2014	☐ Y ☐ N
CO. D JENKINS	LWLIES EDIT DEPT.	21.08.2014	☐ Y ☐ N
			☐ Y ☐ N
			☐ Y ☐ N
			☐ Y ☐ N
			☐ Y ☐ N
			☐ Y ☐ N

LWL 18082014
PAGE NUMBER 8 OF 8   054

8

Illustration by David Fincher

I know what the correct answer is to your question but I don't necessarily believe it. You have those that say you should have tight cohesion across all your platforms and that these platforms have to speak to one another and have to be part of an obvious and visible brand, but I don't necessarily believe that. Then you have the other side where there's this feeling that maybe you should be giving people different experiences on the different platforms. I think I fall somewhere in the middle.

With *Little White Lies* we have slightly different tones on each platform. The magazine is generally a bit more serious—playful, but generally serious. The website is more of a place where we can have a balance between playfulness and seriousness, so it gives us the chance to totally flip from one way to the other. I think the internet is a place where being funny does sometimes pay off and it's worth showing that you have that side to your brand. I don't want it to seem like we're not taking movies seriously, but instead of going on about a rubbish film and writing about why it's rubbish, we could engage with the film in a more amusing way. Take for instance, our deputy editor Adam went to see a film called *Into the Woods*, which is a big musical extravaganza, and he ended up writing a sing-along review. The review is written as lyrics to a song. It's in the spirit of the film since it's a musical, but it's critiquing it in a slightly different form. So to me that's what unites the platforms—saying the same things but in slightly different ways.

What can you tell me about distribution? You're obviously worldwide.

In general I think distribution is really, really tough. It's like this really difficult equation that everyone has a different answer to—and nobody is right and nobody is wrong. If you want to get the magazine out there quick and wide you have to pay for it.

Although we're available in the US and Europe, the magazine is printed here in the UK, so sometimes it takes longer than we'd like for our US readers to get issues. Our readers somewhat take distribution for granted, where the thinking is that the mag should be in certain places at certain times, but it's not as easy as that.

Are you working with one distribution company or is it several?

We currently work with one company that has an international network of local distributors.

How many people do you have working full-time in-house?

TCOLondon is the name of the media company who publishes the magazine. The company prints *Little White Lies* and another magazine called *Huck*, which focuses on youth and DIY culture. We also work on other client projects and create audio, video, and design projects as well as consult for brands. Currently there are about twenty-four people who work across the two titles. We've got an art team, a design team, a commercial team, a video team, and an editorial director as well. Adam Woodward is the digital editor, focusing his attention on our website, a new weekly app which offers a digest of the magazine, and various other projects. Our staff writer is Sophie Monks Kaufman who came into the world of film journalism pretty untested but proved herself to be an exemplary writer and interviewer. Then there's the design team: Timba Smits is design maestro who has very detailed knowledge of print, type, illustration, design, just about everything really. Also the lead designer on the magazine is Laurène Boglio who has this incredible, evocative, and playful drawing style that translates perfectly in print and digital—she's an amazing gif maker too. Then there's Oliver Stafford who works mainly on the crisper, cleaner *Huck*, but, again is super-talented and can adapt his style to anything going. D'Arcy Doran is our head of content and he oversees everything we put out to make sure it meets the high standard we've created for ourselves—call it quality control if you will.

Is your major revenue stream from the magazine itself or is it from the other avenues that you've mentioned?
It's from the other avenues.

Is the magazine actually profitable?
Although we don't disclose financial details, we're happy with how things are going. We've got good momentum.

How do you go about getting advertisers? Do they come to you or do you go to them?

Do you select certain brands? How does that all come together?
We're still getting a feel for this shift in the advertising market that's taken place, but yes, it happens in a variety of ways. Sometimes people will get in contact with us, sometimes it's vice versa. We're trying to be a bit more proactive about it and get the magazine under people's noses so we can get those conversations started.

Do you have a salesperson on board?
Yes. His job is generally to make contact with people in the advertising world.

What would you say is the most challenging part of running a magazine?
I am going to be lame and say just trying to maintain the quality with the time and budget that we have. Just trying to create something that I feel is worthy of people's time, attention, and money, really. It can be tough trying to come up with original ideas and put them into specific contexts, so I think the biggest challenge is trying to keep the quality at a level that reflects the brand as a whole.

What do you find most rewarding? What makes you feel good?
Definitely those special days when the truck pulls up to our office and the first copies of the mag arrive. There's a little ritual where everyone gets up from their chairs and forms a daisy chain from the back of the van and we bring the magazines into the office that way. Then there's this really nice "break open the box and

hand out copies" moment. Most of us tend to just hold it up and smell it before we even open it. Then you have this brief feeling of euphoria, you flip through a few pages, but then it's back to work. Funny enough, we get a lot of comments on how much people love the smell of the magazine.

What things do you feel most contribute to the success of a magazine?

I can only speak from my personal taste, but I am someone who really values journalism and ideas and the ways in which people articulate themselves and the fact that they're being given an outlet for their passion. For me a successful edition of our magazine is when it's visible that there are a lot of passionate people who are speaking in very articulate terms. I am not in this profession to get rich or anything like that, and I'm aware that I'm very lucky to have enough money to be able to watch loads of movies and write about them, all things which I love to do.

What about failure? If I were starting out what would you say I really need to concentrate on or look out for?

If I was to start a new magazine tomorrow, all of my energies would be focused on making that first edition like a bomb, basically—and I don't mean that in a negative way.

Yes, I understand.

Yes, something that's going to be easy and obvious on what it's about and why it exists.

Also, since the magazine is the product, I'd want to be thinking about how I could sell and market it. I'd be thinking about what its function would be just as much as actually creating the magazine itself. It's not just a case of, "This isn't being done anywhere else so we should do it," or a case of just following something you believe in your heart. I think you have to be quite objective, look at it rather coldly and ask yourself, "Does the world really need this?"

Asking those hard questions about the inception of the magazine, or the inception of anything, is nine times out of ten going to make you improve it and hone it—and there's even a small chance that you might think, "Actually no, this is not going to work." But you shouldn't overanalyze the situation to the point where you're going to convince yourself not to move forward, because you can second-guess yourself to death and then you'll end up doing nothing—there also has to be that factor in which a leap of faith is involved. But I think you should spend a long time talking about it with people who have knowledge on the subject and who share similar sensibilities and just say, "Hey, this is the idea, what do you think?" Ask them to be quite brutal with their response.

What kinds of skills would you say are vital for a magazine editor or publisher to have in today's publishing environment?

I don't really have that much contact with other editors or publishers, but from what I do know, everyone has a different way of working and it's

9 771745 916048

Issue 56   Nov/Dec '94   £6

Little White Lies

Truth & Movies

1 9 9 4

MUTUAL APPRECIATION

DAVID MICHÔD AND GUY PEARCE CANDIDLY REFLECT ON THE SHARED CULTURAL
MOTIFS THAT INFORMED BOTH *ANIMAL KINGDOM* AND *THE ROVER*.

INTERVIEW BY ADAM WOODWARD ILLUSTRATION BY LAURÉES ROSILIO

Image 1: DAVID MICHÔD

Image 2: GUY PEARCE

Image 3: A DOG

Image 4: MELBOURNE

Image 5: GUY PEARCE IN *THE PROPOSITION*

Image 6: GUY PEARCE'S FACIAL HAIR

Image 7: MEL GIBSON AS MAD MAX

Image 8: NED KELLY

Image 9: THE STONE ROSES' 'SECOND COMING'

Illustration by Guy Pearce

pretty much people just improvising. I mean, I have no formal training as an editor and everything I do is essentially inspired by the editor I worked with at *Time Out*.

Although it's a simple thing to say, I think it's important to understand what your goal is. Understand what your desired end point looks like for everything you do. And I don't mean that as a way to gauge if something has been a success or a failure, but you need to be able to know why you're doing what you're doing.

I also think it's important to stay abreast of everything that's happening in the world. Our publisher Vince Medeiros makes it a point to keep abreast of what's going on in the publishing world. If you're a publisher working in any form of media—whether it be websites, social media, books, just anything—then it's important that you know what's happening, what's out there, who's innovating, why their innovations have been successful, how they can be improved on, or whether there's a new spin on something that's old.

Do you have some words of wisdom or something inspiring to leave with a reader who may be looking at starting a magazine?
Err…I am trying to think of something that's not negative [laughs]. I would say if there's someone out there who is thinking of starting their own publication, try and think about how it will exist on multiple platforms, because my belief now is that I don't think a magazine can

really exist as just one entity. It has to exist as five different things—maybe they are different or maybe they are the same, but it's important to comprehend that the idea of actually making a magazine is very antiquated now. It's a case of trying to think beyond the page and creating something that fits into a larger framework.

I understand. Is there anything you feel I left out or you'd like to add?
Yes. Talking of brand extensions, this year we collaborated with Faber & Faber and did a book called *What I Love About Movies*, a deluxe coffee table book, which is just one example of how you can amplify your brand. We've been talking a lot in terms of platforms where you have to create content, but for magazines now, and for us in particular, we're focused on programming, we're focused on events, and different physical-type things that gives us the opportunity to actually interact with our audience. Although it's time consuming and involves a lot of hard work, it's also vital to our survival as a publication.

PAPER

scandalous fashion

astonishing beauties

amazing tattoos

astounding style

crazy couture

plus:
revolutionary women
dressed drastically

Sept. 2005

SHOCK
+ AWE

THE RADICAL FASHION ISSUE

11

PAPER

DAVID HERSHKOVITS

Magazine name: *PAPER*
Founder and publisher: David Hershkovits
Year founded: 1984
Tagline: More than a magazine
Editorial mission: To break the internet
Location: New York, USA
Website: papermag.com
Formats: Print, blog, and digital
Issues per year: Eight
Language: English
Reach: Worldwide
Available: Website, digital newsstands, newsstands, bookstores, and independent stores
Circulation: 125,000
Price per issue: $10 USD
One-year subscription: $9.99 USD
Size of in-house team: Forty

Lorraine: Hi David, what did you do before you started *PAPER* magazine?
David: Well, we launched *PAPER* thirty years ago now, and prior to that I had been working in New York at a publication called *Soho Weekly News*, which was a guide to events that took place in the downtown area back in the late seventies. At the time, there was another weekly called the *Village Voice*, which was very successful but kind of old school and more hippie-like, as it had come out of the alternative press scene. *Soho Weekly News* was a little more contemporary—we were more punk rock, featuring a lot of fashion and much more visual—almost like an updated version of the *Village Voice*. And for a while there we were the two competing downtown weeklies.

Soho Weekly eventually folded and started going through different hands. New York City was bankrupt at the time and it wasn't a good time for any kind of business. Big parts of the city, like the Bronx and the East Village where I was, had burned down and New York was not the friendly place that you would think of today. As a result there was a lot of traction from people all over the world who were excited by the idea of living in New York because it was so cheap back then—the opposite of what it is now.

With all these people from different parts of the world, a bubbling scene of creativity developed in the '80s that we were very much a part of—we had friends like Keith Haring, Robert Mapplethorpe, Willie Smith, and Kenny Scharf, people who we'd now consider legends —living and working downtown in those times. My business partner, Kim Hastreiter, and I believed that there was still a need for a publication that catered to this downtown scene and that's how we came to it really, because *Soho Weekly* folded and we just felt that there was still a need for something like it, so we stuck with the idea.

I understand that *PAPER* literally started out as a piece of paper, not anything like a magazine at all, is that correct?

That is correct. It started out like a foldout poster so when you looked at it you could see it was oversized and when you unfolded it, it turned into this big poster. It was printed in black and white on both sides and the graphics were very pop with big and small pictures alongside short articles. We got our friends, who were the celebrities of the scene back then, to contribute and we charged fifty cents for people to buy it. We created little ads around the edges, almost like a Monopoly board, and charged two hundred and fifty dollars for each one. It ended up amounting to five thousand dollars, which was enough for us to cover the print costs, and that's how we got started.

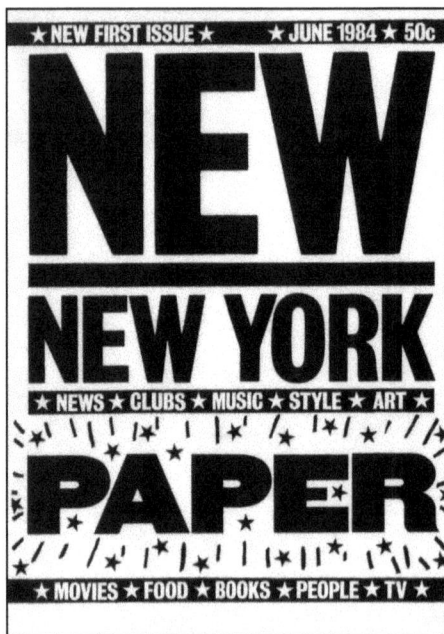

First issue of *PAPER*, 1984

Where did the name *PAPER* come from?

The name *PAPER* arose because we never found a name that everybody really loved but what we did love was the generic side of what we were doing—the whole black-and-whiteness of it. The original logo, which is actually very similar to the current logo, was the generic *PAPER* logo that you might see on the container today. We were also somewhat inspired by agnès b., the fashion brand, as they used lots of black and white in their designs and had this very simple, almost generic approach to fashion. They didn't try to embellish and make big statements, it was almost like they made quiet statements.

How was it that *PAPER* the poster eventually became a magazine?

The process was evolutionary. Because the poster format was obviously limited we could only do so many ads and we needed to figure out how to actually make some money from it, so we ended up inserting a small but more conventional-looking magazine inside the poster and when you opened the poster there was this other piece that would come out. This enabled us to do full-page ads and other things of that nature.

Was the magazine on the inside black and white as well?

Yes, but everything morphed from there. The magazine grew and got bigger to the point where we flipped it and ended up putting the poster inside the magazine. All of our growth was organic, we didn't ever raise a huge amount of money to grow the business in a way that people do today. It was more like a DIY project, but it just kept growing and growing to the point—I think somewhere in the early '90s—that we finally felt we had a substantial enough magazine to do perfect binding along with a full color cover. We were oversized at the time but ended up cutting it back as we didn't feel that we needed to be eccentric to get noticed because it was all about the content, which was different enough by itself anyway. We also wanted to be more conventional for business reasons, mostly for the newsstand and the advertisers, and for the people who were used to creating certain formats that would fit into a regular sized magazine.

If I asked what the secret is to keeping a magazine going for over thirty years and keeping it current over time, what would your answer be?

The number one rule as far as the guide to success is don't give up. That's the reason why we're still here today—we just never stopped. I mean, along the way we have had many bad days and years, and in our case with the economy crumbling, the World Trade Center being attacked, and the internet bubble bursting—as you can imagine over a period of thirty years you go through a lot of economic upheavals, especially with a company like ours that was not really making a lot of money and didn't have the deep pockets to help us survive any of those situations.

This is what we wanted to do and we figured out that we would sacrifice our salaries and just do whatever we had to. When we finally did get salaries, nobody ever made that much, but we wanted to keep the publication going, and fortunately for us enough people got behind and supported the magazine which made it feasible enough for us to sustain it. As far as how do we stay current and all of that, I never really found that to be a problem since it's my nature to be current and on top of the latest artists, bands, movies, fashion, and all the types of things that we write about.

But today, many years later, it's not really possible for any one person to know it all. I can still tell when I hear or see something that I know is going to be really important for one reason or another. We also have our staff—and I feel like we've somewhat raised a generation over the thirty years, not just here but in general, that we've taught how to look at the world around them and helped them to identify a lot of what has since become everyday, but in our time, thirty years ago, that wasn't the case. It's the same with indie films or indie music or all the hip-hop that everyone now takes for granted—at one time it was just a small group of people and somebody had to stand up and say this is really good and cool and fun, lets support it. That's what we were doing along the way. I feel that we helped the culture along in the direction that we would have liked to see it go, and that's one of the rewards of doing something like this.

I read somewhere that you said—and sorry for not quoting you directly—but I read that you said you were more interested in giving exposure to up-and-coming artists as opposed to household names that everybody was already familiar with. Has that changed somewhat, or do you still have that same outlook for the magazine?

Yes, that has changed somewhat. But along the lines of the ethos and the culture behind the magazine and the whole company in general, we still get way more excited by something we feel is going to be really amazing, as at the end of the day, that's what really moves us.

But given the changes in the medium (in particular in terms of technology and the internet making so much information accessible all the time), we feel like a lot of the world that we were in tune with—relating to new things that might be going on in the city or in the culture—is out there all the time now. Everybody is constantly trying to discover new things and tell other people about them. So in that respect we feel that the world has caught up to us, but that's also been very liberating because when that happened it enabled us to say, "Okay, well if they're all going to be in our world, then we're going to be in theirs too." And at that time we decided to start paying more attention to the mass culture but using our point of view to reflect exactly how we relate to it.

So in answer to your question, we wouldn't necessarily just throw someone on the cover because they're famous, we would try and do something with them to make it more like *PAPER*, where there would always be some type of edge to it. Even in the famous world there are people I would describe as "bland famous" [laughs] and then there's the ones I'd consider more outrageous. Here at *PAPER* we tend to gravitate towards the more outrageous.

As far as the internet and social media, although most of the independent magazines I've interviewed so far have not been running as long as you have, I've noticed that a lot of them are trying to find the ideal mix of content as far as what they print in the magazine and what they give away for free online. How do you handle that at *PAPER*?

Well that's something that we're constantly talking about, because as you said, nobody really knows how to do it, so we're all trying to figure it out and see what works best. I don't really feel like we're giving anything away if we publish online at the same time.

Typically in the past, stories would come out in the magazine first and then as time went on we would then release some of those stories online. So there'd be a mix online of original content that was generated on a daily basis as well as content from the magazine, where the stories and visuals take a lot more time to create. But with the recent Kim Kardashian issue we had to switch it all around because the material was so hot we were worried that it would get out there before *we* could get it

PAPER

NEW YORK WINTER 2014 $10

BREAK THE INTERNET
KIM KARDASHIAN

PAP ER

IT'S A
**NICKI
MINAJ**
WORLD
(WE JUST LIVE IN IT)

**AI
WEI WEI**
JAKE SHEARS
ON **CHROME**
HEARTS
**MARIA
SHARAPOVA**

12
WHO
RULE
L.A.

STYLE:
**COW-
BOYS**
AND

out—whether from the printer, somebody on the newsstand, or whoever it was—there are lots of ways it could have been leaked before we were ready. So in that case we decided to put those images out online weeks before they were at the newsstand.

It turned out to be quite amazing, because people read all kinds of things into it and wrote articles about how we had changed the face of publishing and this was going to be the future of publishing. Now, I don't know if that's really going to be the future of publishing but it definitely got people thinking about things in a very different way. It also made us see the power of what a magazine could do online.

To me a magazine is like a movie, it's something that takes a long time to create. It's not like a story that you throw up online on a blog or something, so it should be treated like a movie. It should have its own marketing plan and a whole strategy developed around how it's going to be released. What are you going to release? What else are you going to do with the content? Will you turn it into a movie? Will it be a TV show? What else?

Typically with a magazine once it's published it's done, it's over and everybody moves on to the next issue, but my perspective is that when it's published that's only the beginning. The heavy lifting is creating the product and getting it out, there's a lot of work involved, it's a labor-intensive project, so really that should just be the beginning of whatever you have to do. You can actually learn something from the big marketers and the advertisers who are always looking to continue the story. So when the story's out it's not the end, it's like, well how do we continue the story? How do you keep this Kim Kardashian story going? What is "break the internet"? How do you manifest that in other ways? Social is a big way of doing that, so in that sense social media becomes your friend. For a long time people were afraid that the technology would kill print, but I feel that most companies should have figured out by now that it could actually help, and that's how you should be looking at it, as a tool to help you rather than something to be afraid of.

What advice would you give to other publishers as far as using the internet to their best advantage?
I think they need to think of it as a complement to whatever they're doing. They should look at it as an extension of the magazine. It's not enough just to take those stories and publish them online. They have to do more because the internet allows you to do video and to actually be social with your audience. Then there are all these platforms and distribution channels that can be used as different ways to distribute various types of content which, when you think about it, is really great for a publisher today.

Now how you monetize and make money from all that? That's a whole other question, but in terms of becoming relevant, it's very important for print to be relevant which can be very difficult because we're always late to the game as far as some new story that's happening. So I think you have to be online, you have to be a digital brand where the magazine is only part of your distribution platform but it's not *the* distribution platform.

As for your business model, is the magazine your main source of income or do you generate income from other areas that are related to the magazine?

Over the years we started another component to the business called ExtraExtra. ExtraExtra is a marketing company that could also be described as a service provider. What we do there is work with the big brands to help them connect with our demographic—that could be by doing a live event and inviting the right type of people, helping them with their social media by creating multimedia content such as videos and the like, or just in general, taking the skills that we've learned over the years and helping them to use and apply some of the strategies that might work well for their business.

So there's the magazine, the website, and then this particular division that's doing very well, maybe even a little better than the magazine. But that's going to change over the next year or so because we expect digital to grow dramatically and become a much bigger component of the business as we continue to develop our products and ideas we have on some new things we'd like to do.

What do you find the most challenging part of running a magazine?

Given that the answer to that will change over time, today I would say the financial aspect, because we've never had the luxury of a big bank account to fall back on in order to take advantage of some of the opportunities we've had along the way. But at the same time it's been fabulous and I'm not saying that I regret it, but I do feel like there were opportunities that we couldn't take advantage of—but then that really just made us keep our focus on the magazine. But yes, the financial aspect is the hardest part, after that would come managing people and getting the most out of them.

How many full-time staff do you have?

Roughly about forty people all together. We have people that come in to help out with deadlines in certain areas and we have freelancers that work in our ExtraExtra division that come in when we have a lot of work and need additional people for various jobs.

What's the most rewarding? What makes you feel good and why have you continued to do this now for thirty years?

Well, this is something I love to do and it's what I do [laughs]. For me personally the best is still writing—I started out as a writer and I still feel that's the best thing that I can do and something that makes me the happiest when I'm doing it. I still write for the magazine and on other projects as well. I think the other thing is having been there to support a lot of people in

PAPER

30TH ANNIVERSARY ISSUE BROOKE CANDY

their early days when they were starting out—seeing them go on to success and seeing the appreciation they have for us and what we've done; being there for them when they needed the help, that's a great feeling. Also it's rewarding to know that we had something to do with the world that we're in today.

What factors do you think contribute to the success of a magazine? What have you seen over the years?

A magazine is also a business. It's like a corporation with huge staffs and budgets and its own agenda. But that's very different from what we do, because we had a community that we always felt we were very much a part of. Even today when that community doesn't exist physically in the sense that it did then, we still feel that it's out there—it's more dispersed but it exists in places like London and China and many other parts of the world. The people were always what we were about, but the hard part in print is clearly trying to be relevant when everything is digital.

You're working on something that takes months to create and then it comes out and it's immediately old [laughs]. So it's a challenge to say the least, but I think that magazines will continue to be with us, they're beautiful as objects, and also a fantastic delivery system of information, photography, illustration, design, and even advertising. Advertisers have those photo shoots that cost them so much money to produce and it just doesn't look as good online.

Magazines today are becoming like couture products—they're expensive and take a lot to create. Advertising was there to support it for all those years, so it sold for a relatively small amount because the return wasn't based on the sales, it was based on the advertising. But that's changed now and since there's not enough advertising, what happens then is that you have to raise the price of the magazine. I feel as the advertising drops, the expense of creating a magazine has to be carried by the cover price, and as you can see, if you go to the stores the prices of print publications keep going up.

I think they also look considerably better as well. I was quite surprised by the standard that I found on the newsstand. It's amazing.

Yes, especially if you're looking at foreign magazines, they are costing anywhere from twenty to thirty dollars here.

What factors do you think contribute to the failure of a magazine? What have you witnessed over the years?

Ultimately, you have to stay relevant to your audience. But I think you have to have a strong point of view that makes you stand out and gives you a reason for existing besides just being a business venture. There needs to be a cause or some type of belief system behind it, the product needs to have inherent values that people can connect with.

What skills or disciplines you think are important for a magazine publisher to have?

If I said to you that I wanted to publish a magazine, what would you say is important for me to know, have, or do?

Gee, I would say everything. I don't feel like anybody can really put himself or herself into a silo anymore and just study one thing and expect to go out into the world and work, because things are just overlapping onto one another right now.

You have to understand business, you have to understand people, and you have to understand writers and how they think. Creative people are very different from business people, so if you can be a bridge between the two that's amazing, but typically most publishers are not like that. Today publishers are the business people, they are there to make sure the business runs well and for the most part they're kept separate from the editorial. But I don't think that's a good formula for today because it's not working—so they need to be able to understand it all. It's a very complicated time.

Can you leave me with a last message of wisdom or inspiration for someone who might be contemplating starting a publication?

If you're passionate about a subject, whatever it may be, whether it's skateboarding, snowboarding, or being a rapper—anything—there's always room for something like a magazine to be in that industry where you can get to express your love or passion for a subject, after all that's where it all starts. But you have to really, really love it because otherwise you're not going to make it. You're going to give up and it just won't be a good experience for you. And lastly, definitely don't go into it because you want to make money.

SNEAKER ☆ FREAKER
www.sneakerfreaker.com
KE REJUVEN8

14
ISSUE
MADE IN
MELBOURNE
$10 (inc gst)

SNEAKER
FREAKER
www.sneakerfreaker.com
ACG ASHIKO FLYWIRE BOOT

15
ISSUE
MADE IN
MELBOURNE
$10 (inc gst)

SNEAKER FREAKER

SIMON "WOODY" WOOD

12

Magazine name: *Sneaker Freaker*
Founder and editor: Simon "Woody" Wood
Year founded: 2002
Tagline: Keep your laces loose
Editorial mission: To boldly go where no sneaker magazine has gone before
Location: Melbourne, Australia
Website: sneakerfreaker.com
Formats: Print, blog, and books
Issues per year: Three
Languages: English, German, Russian, and Spanish
Reach: Worldwide
Available: Website, limited newsstands, and sneaker boutiques
Circulation: 25,000 (English version only)
Price per issue: $8.00 AUD (approx. $7 USD)
One-year subscription: $35 AUD (approx. $31 USD)
Size of in-house team: Five full-time

Lorraine: Hi Woody, tell me a little bit about your background.

Woody: I studied media studies at RMIT University, here in Melbourne, and was involved in a lot of the extra curricular activities. It was a great experience because it gave me exposure to a really wide variety of disciplines and I ended up being deeply immersed in the political machinery of the university itself. In my first few years I had a budding career in commercial radio and was convinced I had my working future all mapped out for me.

Was this DJing or doing something like talk radio?

Not exactly. I was doing the graveyard shift at the local underground radio station. I produced commercials and got to make news documentaries. In my spare time I also recorded bands. Radio was never something I explicitly set out to do, but I developed an interest in the technology and caught some lucky breaks that really opened doors quickly for me, which made the industry that much more appealing.

But all that changed when I was elected to be the coeditor of *Catalyst*, the student newspaper at RMIT. When I first saw the Apple Mac (as we called it back then) I had a total epiphany—before that I had no idea that I wanted to be a graphic designer, but once I was exposed to QuarkXPress that was it for me. Prior to that my total computer experience had been limited to the Commodore 64, so seeing the Apple just blew my mind. It was a super-creative machine that you could use to actually "make stuff"—the Mac changed the whole game for me.

Doing the newspaper was brilliant. I learned how to stay up late and survive on flavored milk and cold pizza. We used a bromide camera and manually pasted up the pages. We did color work by hand with scalpels—it was crazy. We had absolutely no idea what we were doing but we learned fast.

When I graduated, there was absolutely no work anywhere in Melbourne, so I decided to move to London. At the time I was one of the very few people who knew anything about typesetting on the Mac, so I managed to parlay the little bit of skill I had—along with a fair amount of BS—and ended up walking straight into a cushy advertising job.

So how did *Sneaker Freaker* come about?
Magic! One day out of the blue I just thought, "What about doing a sneaker magazine? I'll get loads of Nikes for free!" And that was the start of *Sneaker Freaker* back in 2002.

Did you do any market research or create a business plan prior to launching?
I think you know the answer to that [laughs]. I thought about it for a few days and then took about a week to put the first issue together. I didn't have a business plan then and still don't to this day.

What kind of freedom does that allow you?
Well, it's a beautifully naive way to approach things and it means that you don't have any enormous expectations to live up to. It's not the smartest method, but who needs a business plan when you're just one person? From the start *Sneaker Freaker* just took off and I've basically been struggling to hold on to the reins ever since.

I understand that you initially held a launch party—how did it go?

The launch party was amazing. I told people in true word-of-mouth style and a few hundred showed up. This was pre-Facebook and Twitter days and I don't even think we had a website built yet, so I rang my friends and put flyers out in all the stores—that's how you had to do it back then, in the olden days [laughs].

At the time, I worked at a club called Revolver, so we had our party there, and that helped to bring in the crowd too. Journalists were amazed and I received an enormous amount of press. I must have done about a hundred interviews with all the major newspapers and fashion magazines—it was surreal. *Sneaker Freaker* was just me working from my home, but they really thought it was a legitimate organization and all of a sudden I became a world-class expert. They probably also thought I was nuts and that it would all be over in a few months' time.

Was all the attention just from local press?
Yes, it was local at first, but it quickly became international once the global media got hold of this "crazy Imelda Marcos sneaker guy from Australia" story. *The New York Times* emailed me to come in, they must have thought I lived in Manhattan or something. But I quickly informed them that it would take me about thirty hours to get there.

What did your first issue look like?
It was pretty raw. Not a sophisticated thing at all, but I consciously tried to make it a true fanzine. It wasn't produced in a conventional

manner—I wasn't trying to make it look like a "real" magazine. I was trying to make it look like it was created by someone who just loved sneakers and was doing it purely for the love.

How did you come up with your magazine's name *Sneaker Freaker*?

It just popped up. I can't say I ever had a different name in mind. I didn't particularly love it or hate it, but I didn't have anything better. There's a certain symmetry to it and of course the fact that it rhymes doesn't hurt. Designing the logo was a nightmare though—it was one of the first things I ever did. Two words, seven letters long, and they're almost identical. Easy! I flipped the "Freaker" upside down, which also went along with the whole "down under" thing.

Very clever.

Thanks for saying that—I just made it up! [laughs]. It's funny how some of these random ideas just work out. There are lots of brands with strange names but your name just becomes you after a while and I think everyone eventually stops analyzing it. If you think about it, all the great company names are often five letters or less because they make the best logos—they're simple and easy to remember.

When you initially created the fanzine, was there anything more to the vision than that? Were you even thinking about an issue two or three?

Issue 1 was definitely about as far ahead as I was thinking. In fact, I hadn't even thought about how I would distribute the magazine, but I ended up sending them to a few stores that gave them away for free. It's funny, those issues are now worth somewhere around three to four hundred dollars apiece.

Really?

Yeah, crazy money. I wish I had a box of them. The first issue was free and years later the current issues are still being stolen because people still think that they're a giveaway, but they haven't been free for thirteen years [laughs].

What made you decide to make the magazine in such a compact size?

I went and spoke to a store prior to creating the first issue and they said, "Whatever you do, don't make it too big, because we've got to put them on the counter." That proved to be valuable insight because A5 is incredibly efficient and has got to be the cheapest size you can make a magazine in. As an export business—which is what we've now become—if I'd made it twice the size I would've had to put up our prices by 40–50 percent to cover shipping and the other costs as well.

How would you describe your audience?

It's basically just anyone who loves sneakers. The age range is from twelve to fifty with the sweet spot being right in the middle.

I like to think that *Sneaker Freaker* is like a trade union for sneaker collectors. We're the middleman between the brands and the kids. We call the brands out when they're not on point—I mean, we'll be as honest as we can, but at the same time I'm very much aware that this is a commercial enterprise. We're always on the edge and I think our audience understands the position we're in. Brands also know that we do a great job of explaining what is going on in their world as well.

Would it be fair to say that your readership is male-dominated?
Yes.

What percentage are we talking about?
Ninety percent, maybe higher.

As a pioneer in your category, how do you manage to stay prominent with all the different types of media that are available now?
You just gotta stay one step ahead. I'd like to think that we are respected for being the first sneaker magazine out there, but primarily I hope we're known for the quality of the content we create. I'm still super hands-on. I edit every single word, I'm personally responsible for every single thing in the magazine. If there's a mess-up, I own it. If you love it, I take your compliment as well. I am personally highly invested in every aspect of the magazine.

So you're the actual editor too?
Essentially the magazine is me. I maintain not just the quality, but also the progressive direction. I'm the benevolent dictator, I can't let go, I'm a control freak [laughs].

I noticed that you get over a million visits to your site every month. The level of engagement in your forum and on your Facebook and Twitter pages is extremely high.
Yeah, our Facebook is out of control. The comments are brilliant. It's funny to read what our audience thinks—good and bad. The brands don't always appreciate the honesty though.

Who administers your social accounts?
There are five of us in the office, two do Instagram and Twitter, but all of us contribute to Facebook. We're not using Google+ at the moment though. Facebook is our biggest audience—we'll have a million followers soon. We're getting up to 30,000 likes on some posts, sometimes even as high as 90,000. Facebook seems to like us and our audience seems to like what we do, so we're seeing an incredible amount of growth there.

How is the content in the magazine different from what appears on your website?
The magazine is about two hundred pages long and about one hundred of those consist of longform features. We might have a thirty-page story on one single shoe or one collector. In issue 28 we had a seventy-page story on the Nike Air Max franchise and it was easily the most successful story we've ever done. I see those features as the antithesis of the web mentality, where you use 140 characters or less, then swiftly move on to the next topic. I feel it's the equivalent of junk food—it makes you happy for five seconds but it's not satisfying.

SNEAKER FREAKER™

ISSN 1833-6884

ISSUE **32**

MADE IN MELBOURNE A$10 (INC. GST)

ADIDAS ORIGINALS
SUPERSTAR

LOVE LETTER TO A MASTERPIECE

I think many magazines have made an error by breaking everything up into these tiny little chunks of information. My favorite magazine is *Vanity Fair* because they have incredible features in every issue. I learn something from every one—useful information on Ebola and white-collar crime and international polo jetsetters. The only thing I don't like about *Vanity Fair*'s layout is that they make you flip to another page to read the next section of a feature and then flip right to the back of the book for the last bit of the story—but that's just my personal gripe.

With the website content, the shorter the better seems to be king these days. I hate that. We actually stopped publishing our magazine content online because we were just giving it away. Other sites would steal our content and claim it as their own, which drives me nuts. They don't just take a photo here and there, they'll also take the five thousand words we've written and stick it up on their website with absolutely no attribution, as if they wrote the whole thing themselves. That's what's messed up about the web—there's no recourse for that.

I'm also conscious of the fact that what we're writing is essentially a form of contemporary history. What we say in print is the only proof of anything happening in our niche world of sneakers. It becomes the truth, and it has a shelf life that may even outlast my involvement in the magazine.

I was in Manchester recently and people were asking me about stories from as far back as Issue 4, which was over a decade ago. That stuff is memorable to our audience even eight or nine years later—it's timeless, they nerd out on it. But with website content no one can remember what happened fifteen minutes ago. People have to really focus on a magazine, but when they're surfing the web looking at sites they're often doing a million other things at the same time.

You're right. Do the people on your team wear all hats and jump in wherever they fit in, or do you all have specific roles?
We have specific roles but we cross over on just about everything. We have one graphic designer who is also the main photographer. The other guys know how to take photos for Instagram, and then I do everything from taking photos to designing the pages and designing the shoes that we put out as *Sneaker Freaker* collaborations.

So you still do the layout?
For some stories yes, because I like to. I feel that if I ever stop I'll lose those skills, and being a control freak, at the end of the day I want it to look the way I want it to look. We make the effort to redesign the magazine every time we do it so no two editions ever look the same. We use different typefaces in every issue—as we only do shoes it can get repetitive so I'm very conscious of that.

It must be quite challenging to work without an in-house style guide.

Yes, it can be a creative challenge at times but I like to keep it pretty unstructured. It's certainly looking a lot more professional these days. Sometimes I tell the team, "Man, we've got to loosen up, it's looking a bit too corporate, let's do something crazy," but they have absolutely no idea what I'm talking about most of the time [laughs].

Do you use freelancers or is it basically just the five of you?

Yes, we use freelancers and we have extra people that come in to do specific jobs as well. But I edit everything at a micro level because it just drives me nuts to see something that could have been better, sharper, maybe funnier, or more accurate. What I've realized is that it's better to be self-sufficient. I would like to have more input from outside people, but you've got to have a certain amount of confidence that you're in charge. You need to keep challenging your audience, not just giving them what they expect. I want them to be surprised by at least one thing in each issue, plus provide them with something they knew absolutely nothing about. It's all about balance.

Could you briefly go over the whole process from planning the table of contents to finishing the final layout?

Actually, we only had our first table of contents in Issue 28 because we had a spare page and I thought I should probably finally do one after a decade. We also don't have page numbers, which drives our German office crazy. I really don't see the point and will never have page numbers in the magazine.

When putting together an issue we rely on people all around the world to send us the shoes, so the magazine happens very piecemeal. Shoes turn up, we photograph them, and we keep going until it's finished. We discover projects—some we're not supposed to know about—we beg marketing people to send us shoes, we threaten to ignore them, we cajole them, we bribe them with promises of the cover—whatever it takes. It's an ongoing process that is getting more and more complicated because we have to stay a few steps ahead of the digital competition. At the end of the day, every magazine wants the same thing—they want to feature the freshest content. It's a tough world.

As far as distribution, how did you end up going from launch party to being sold in over fifty countries?

I think it's a bit like playing Tetris really—all the blocks came down and literally just fell into place. It took a long time. I had a lot to learn about international freight and the magazine distribution business in general since it's not written down anywhere I could find. There's nowhere you can go and learn that stuff unless you get a job somewhere and then take that knowledge with you. The big breakthrough came when we made a *Sneaker Freaker* book that sold exceptionally well all around the world. It opened a lot of doors for us, especially in the US.

With distribution did you select the areas you wanted to be in, then find the main distributors there and just call them up?
Initially, I was only thinking about Australian stores, but when the second issue came out I received a call from a store in Paris called Colette. I didn't even know who they were, but it turns out that they are seriously the coolest store in the world [laughs]. As luck would have it, they were our first international stockist. I think what makes Colette amazing is that they were out there looking for things and they saw something in *Sneaker Freaker* that they thought was interesting. They didn't know who I was—and the fact that I'm Australian is a whole other conversation.

Anyway, I went down to the post office and asked how much would it be to send fifty magazines to Paris. They said three hundred dollars and I was like, "They're not gonna pay that much!" So that was a big problem I had to solve.

The frustrating thing for start-ups is that you need to get everything up to a certain number so the economies of scale can kick in and work in your favor. Of course with international freight the more you send the cheaper it gets, but that's no comfort when you're just sending the odd box out here and there. Over time all those types of problems have been solved but it was quite a slow process.

Is *Sneaker Freaker* available on newsstands?
Not really. It doesn't really make sense for us. It requires too much capital to buy into that caper, and as the magazine is so compact I think we'd get lost on the shelf. Saying that, we actually do great business with Barnes and Noble in the US and we used to be huge in Borders before it went bust. I'm really happy with our distribution—we now have European and American agents who sell it to the top-echelon sneaker boutiques, which is where we belong. None of those stores have magazine accounts, so it's a unique system that we've managed to build up over the years.

Have you ever considered creating an app of the magazine?
Yeah, we previously made an app for the iPad and it's the one mistake I regret.

Really?
I mean I've made mistakes, but it's *the* one. It was a speculative thing, we did it, and it turned out to be a total failure.

Why was it a mistake?
I probably shouldn't say it was a mistake, because if I hadn't done it I would always be wondering whether I should have and what it could have turned out to be. We spent quite a bit of time working out how it would work and made what I thought was a pretty good app.

SNEAKA
AFRIKA ™

ISSN 1833-6884

ISSUE
32

MADE IN MELBOURNE A$10 (INC. GST)

ADIDAS 'CITY OF GOLD' ZAFLUX
SOUTH AFRICA
LIMITED EDITION

I really liked *Sneaker Freaker* on the iPad, but like I said, it turned out to be a failure.

Was there interactivity?
Yes, we had some pretty cool stuff with video and interactive features. We invested quite a bit into the way it worked. We certainly didn't just throw up a PDF. The photos on the Retina iPad looked incredible. I remember thinking, "This is better than paper!" because it looked like you could just dive right into the image—it looked amazing.

We created a video cover that looked like a picture of a shoe, but a hand would come in, grab it, and put another in its place. Those are the types of things you can do with digital. The potential excited me, because with paper it's static but with video the door was wide open. Mind you, I never felt the same creative thrill from making the app that I still get when the first copy of the magazine comes back from the printers. Maybe it has something to do with the smell of the ink.

What happened with the app in the end?
I asked every marketing person at every brand I work with, "Are you interested in supporting our digital version, I would love to have two sponsors to pay for it to exist—we'll give you this, this, and this." Although not a single brand was interested we did it anyway. I think we had about fifty thousand downloads in the first few months, it was going really well, but it was free.

The second issue, we charged a few dollars and sold a few hundred units. In the end we spent a ton of money and ended up making a few hundred bucks. Then as the final straw the company we were working with went bust and all of our data got taken down and lost forever, so it doesn't even exist anymore.

From a creative viewpoint I thought it was a success. It was definitely something to learn from. I shouldn't say it was a mistake but more like an experiment that wasn't successful from a business perspective.

How long ago was that?
Four years ago. I felt it was something we should have been offering our readers as another way to interact with *Sneaker Freaker*, but it turned out that no one wanted to pay for it.

You mentioned designing shoes as *Sneaker Freaker* collaborations. What other activities do you do in addition to the magazine?
Well, ultimately—and inadvertently—*Sneaker Freaker* has become a brand. The magazine is what I call our front door as it's the entry point. It used to say "magazine" underneath our logo on the website but we removed that recently after a site redesign. I mean, a lot of blogs describe themselves as magazines, but in my view, just because you write a blog, that doesn't make you a magazine.

Behind the front door, *Sneaker Freaker* has evolved into a creative agency. We design shoes, we create content for social channels, we put on events, and we do a lot of other "stuff." We're easily the best anywhere in the world in terms of writing about shoes and documenting them from a historical point of view. We've written books for PONY, PUMA, and New Balance—we actually just finished a book for Nike which was a huge success. Sometimes it's written as *Sneaker Freaker* and sometimes it isn't, as often we'll write on behalf of a brand.

We also have our online business, which includes monetizing the website traffic. So that's the *Sneaker Freaker* brand in full, but as you'd expect, everything revolves around shoes.

So what are your major revenue streams and where does the bulk of your money come from? Is it the magazine?
Still the magazine. Digital marketing and creative agency work both earn around the same amount of money over the course of a year, but they fluctuate on a short-term basis.

Digital as far as…?
Everything we do online. All the online editorial we sell, the social packages, the banner ads—all of that is stacked up under digital. It's taken a long time but it's at a point where I don't think we'll ever go backwards, we will continue to grow, however, I don't think digital will overtake the magazine any time soon. We are not rapidly hurtling towards an online-only business where the print magazine becomes less desirable to advertisers or our audience.

Like I said before, the magazine is still what we do. I feel like that's a good story because it's easy for journalists to write that print is dead. It seems like every other week there is a magazine going bust, but *Sneaker Freaker* is proof you can still make money out of print. I don't have any experience working on a general music title but that would be tough right now. General fashion would be tough unless you're the establishment like *Vogue*. Look at their summer issue, the book is like two inches thick and they've got something like three hundred ads in there—it's got to be making an incredible amount of money. They spend a lot making it too, it's an amazing thing to hold in your hands, because there are still a lot of brands that like the idea of being in *Vogue*. Whether it actually sells ten thousand dresses or not—who knows?

Do you set a budget for the magazine?
No, never. I have never made a spreadsheet. We do have to get budgets to add up, but I'm allergic to those things.

What do you consider to be the most challenging part of running a magazine?
Perseverance. Having to front up day after day. You finish an issue and you're really satisfied with it for about two minutes, but as soon as the ink dries you know that you've got to do it all again. There's always been—at least in my experience—a sort of masochistic edge to making magazines. If you haven't got it, get out of the game. Trust me, it's a physical and mental marathon.

We put an enormous amount into each magazine in terms of the photography, the writing, the level of research and creativity. We go beyond the call of duty. I hope people appreciate the commitment to quality, but whether they tell us or not, or whether it's reflected in the sales or not, at least we've made something that we're proud of, which is important.

What ultimately makes you want to get up and go to work every day?
Quite simply, I haven't found anything more interesting to do. Once you've started something this successful it's hard to just slack off. On one level it's amazing that I'm still interested in doing it, but what is rewarding about it is the fact that I'm still connecting with people all over the world. I went from being someone who loved shoes to designing them for brands and traveling around the world business class, talking about them, and having an opinion about an entire industry! [laughs]. I guess being taken seriously is part and parcel of becoming successful but I didn't expect it to be so compelling. It's interesting just going around talking shop, contributing my take on it all, because after all, I am an outsider. I'm in the middle of all the different brands and retailers. I love all the speculation and of course a dose of the hot gossip too.

I'm truly immersed in it. I get to see the things that are coming a long way down the line. It's a unique position to be in, really. Not many people get access to all the product, seeing it all and being taken inside the machine and shown different things. That's the part I'm really into—I still love sneakers. Even though I get hundreds of free pairs each year, I still buy them. It's an incurable sickness.

I'm also fascinated by the business side of the industry too, how sneakers are made and sold and how they are marketed and why New Balance is New Balance and why Nike is always number one and Adidas always number two. The inner workings of this whole industry just fascinates me.

Have you ever felt like giving up?
No, I've never felt like giving up or doing anything else.

Never?
No. I mean, you have bad days. All it takes is a few things to go awry and you feel like the whole world is against you. Then five minutes later something good happens and all of a sudden you're back in the game. That's the true nature of running a business.

I rely on all the marketing people from the brands to support *Sneaker Freaker*, so I am very conscious of delivering value and being an entertaining client. I try to make sure that every dollar we earn we give back times three in value, and I hope that's one of the reasons why we're still around. Not forgetting that we also have a genuine audience to deliver to those brands as well.

SNEAKER FREAKER MAGAZINE PH / FX +6

SNEAKER FREAKER MAGAZINE PH / FX +

That's true, that's important.

Sneaker Freaker is stupidly niched, but when you think about it it's not *that* stupidly niched when you're in a forty-billion-dollar-a-year industry. We don't need a huge chunk of the marketing spend in order to sustain us as an organization.

Why do you think it is that you have managed to stay the course?

In this day and age there's so much stuff that's fabricated. There are a lot of marketing companies out there pretending to make things around street culture—they're basically mercenaries—but *Sneaker Freaker* is for real. Someone with a real point of view makes it, and whether it's me or someone else in the company, there's this feel of humanity about it and a realness that I believe is disappearing fast from the world. Everything has become so bland and corporate.

What do you think contributes to a magazine's failure? I'm sure you've seen your fair share of magazines come and go. Did you notice any factors that led to their demise?

Yes, I noticed two obvious things. One is that their audience lost interest and disappeared, and the other is that there weren't enough brands that were willing to pay to be in there. It's tough to see a magazine you love start to get thinner and thinner and waste away. You literally see them die slowly. I always have it in my mind to make each issue better than the last and I figure if we do that, then we're good.

As far as paying for ads, is that a trial and error type of thing? Do you really know prior to launching that you're going to have advertisers to support the magazine?

Oh yeah, it's remarkably consistent. We just had our highest-earning magazine ever. Most of our clients have supported *Sneaker Freaker* for over a decade. We don't have a sales team that's harassing anyone. It just works.

There you go, looks like print is definitely not dead. But how about in general—let's say for a start-up magazine?

If you ask me, print is definitely not dead. I think if you're going to be a magazine you've got to have someone who wants to consume your product and someone who wants to pay to make it happen. You've got to have both of those things. There are magazines out there that probably don't even have an audience but look really amazing and hit all the buttons in terms of what some advertisers want to associate themselves with, but for *Sneaker Freaker*, it's pretty obvious who our audience is. We've never had an ad from a car company or a beer company—we've had a couple of fashion ads over the years—but it's pretty explicit who we are. I don't know about other magazines, but *Sneaker Freaker* is a true labor of love. We don't have huge overheads so we can still be successful without making millions.

If you look at *Maxim* and *Loaded* and all those UK lads magazines, they were very "of their time" in the '90s, but one by one they've all disappeared. Magazines can be incredibly fashionable, but it can be a double-edged sword because you can go in and out of fashion really quickly.

So what's next for *Sneaker Freaker*? Where do you see your title in a year's time?

I don't anticipate any really dramatic changes over the next twelve months aside from just generally refining things. We've built our distribution back up a little bit and we've got some new ways of connecting stores with brands that have been quite successful. They have been really good innovations actually, sometimes it just takes one little insight to lead to a host of other opportunities.

I'd like to try and find a few more really talented writers to work with so I can step back a little. I need to get back to traveling more. I just came back from Manchester and London and I was in South Africa a week before that. We've just picked up a lot of stores in Japan—*Sneaker Freaker* is popping off there again. So I guess that is the benefit of being around for a while—you get used to the ebbs and flows so there's less panic when something doesn't go your way. You just dust yourself off and get back in there.

What about the different languages? Right now I know you have German, Spanish, and Russian versions—are you planning on adding any more?

Yeah, we thought we'd have another one,

maybe two by now. We have to find the right partner for starters. Funnily enough, *Sneaker Freaker* is the only Australian magazine ever to be translated into foreign languages, which I don't think is a particularly well-known fact, even here. Seeing the first version in German, Spanish, and Russian was immensely satisfying. I guess I can add "international media mogul" to my business card now.

What words of advice do you have for a reader who may be looking at starting a magazine?

I think they should do what every other kid is doing now and learn how to be a barista and grow the best moustache they can [laughs].

In all seriousness—just do it. Make it happen. Don't listen to the naysayers and flakes, they never do anything. You can make this business work if you do it right. There is a fantastic magazine success story here in Australia called *frankie*. They've tapped into this slightly hipster, slightly Etsy-girl kind of demographic where they have amazing articles about knitting and making cakes all mixed in with fashion. It's a great example of a magazine of its time—and you know what?—it's grown really big, to the point where it's bigger than some of the mainstream fashion titles here. So it can be done.

I don't know whether the *Sneaker Freaker* story will be replicated again on an international scale—I never really set out for it to be a business. It was really a series of lucky breaks and coincidences that meant the magazine was

able to flourish. It's a unique story, so if there's any inspiration in that, it's just do it—after all, what's the worst that could happen?

And that's about a wrap, Woody. Did I make you talk too much?

No, I love talking about myself [laughs]. I love talking about shoes, it never gets old. I guess it's weird when it's your own story, but sometimes when you step back a little bit you think, "Wow, that was mental. How the hell did that happen? What was I thinking? Why did I do that?" I've had so much help from people in the industry over the years—some of whom I've

never even met—but I know that their influence was critical in allowing *Sneaker Freaker* to become what it is today.

Do you have any regrets?

While I did make the magazine by myself for a long time, I think my only regret is that I wasn't aggressive enough in the early years to expand and really try to make it bigger quicker. I was quite cautious, which was a good thing, but it was also a bad thing. It's all part of the *Sneaker Freaker* narrative now. You can't beat yourself up about your weaknesses but you can learn from them.

Was that about a level of confidence?

No, I was just zooming along really. I didn't have the vision of what it is now. But you know, saying that, I didn't have a role model either, there wasn't a textbook to follow. I just made it up as I went along.

Woody, I couldn't ask you for anything more. You've been most gracious. Thanks so much.

Oh, my pleasure and good luck with the book. I look forward to seeing it. And I really look forward to reading it. Magazine people are crazy, you have to be. I hope they all give you good interviews!

THINGS &INK

ISSUE 8 £6.95
QUARTERLY MAGAZINE
INDEPENDENT | TATTOO | LIFESTYLE
THINGSANDINK.COM

THE

Illustration

ISSUE

THINGS & INK

ALICE SNAPE

13

Magazine name: *Things & Ink*
Publisher and editor: Alice Snape
Year founded: 2012
Tagline: Independent | Tattoo | Lifestyle
Editorial mission: *Things & Ink* is an independent tattoo magazine that takes an artistic approach to content and challenges misconceptions. We strive to create stunning photo shoots using tattoo artists and people with interesting stories to tell. Carefully curated, the editorial content discusses tattoos against their rich cultural history and current tattoo trends. The magazine is for artists, collectors, and those yet to go under the needle. It allows the reader to discover new artists, products, and ideas that will enrich their tattooed lives. *Things & Ink* is a collector's item for tattoo collectors...it is more than just a magazine, it's a lifestyle.
Location: London, UK
Website: thingsandink.com
Formats: Print and blog
Issues per year: Four
Language: English
Reach: Worldwide
Available: Website and digital newsstands
Circulation: 2,000
Price per issue: £6.95 (approx. $10 USD)
One-year subscription: £13.90 (approx. $21 USD)
Size of in-house team: One part-time

Lorraine: All right Alice, what did you do before you launched your publication?
Alice: I worked in the magazine world as a writer and subeditor for women's magazines. Actually, I still write for them now.

Why did you decide to start a magazine?
Well, I did a masters in publishing at university about nine years ago. For my major project I did some research and found a gap in the market with regard to tattoo magazines. I wrote a full report about it and created a prototype of what I envisioned a new kind of tattoo magazine could look like. All my teachers raved about it, they loved it, and basically I've wanted to do it ever since.

How long was it from when you created your prototype until you actually launched?

Quite a while. When I left university all my tutors were saying, "There's a real need for this, you should do it." I knew it was all very well me doing a project in university, but in reality I had no idea how to viably publish a magazine, so for years I just wrote for other publications. At the time I also created a tattoo blog which was my way of publishing the ideas I had for the magazine as I always had it in the back of my mind that one day I would do it. I wrote on the blog for about two years and started working on the actual magazine about eight months prior to its launch. All the way through though, I kept working in the magazine world.

So when you launched you had already performed market research while at university?
Yes, and I knew that the gap in the market still existed because...well let me back up. The

reason I had even started looking into tattoo magazines was because I really wanted to get one myself.

Was this your first one?
Yes it was. So I started buying tattoo magazines and I thought they were pretty vile, I just didn't think they were for me. They catered more to men and were definitely more in the biker style, leaning toward that lifestyle in general.

So they just didn't appeal to you?
Exactly, and what my market research had revealed was that I couldn't find the magazine that I wanted to read.

Did the blog help you build an audience?
Yeah. The blog built up really, really quickly because the popularity of tattoos online is insane—you wouldn't believe it.

Would people find out about your blog through search engines?
Yes. Plus I was tweeting about it and posting on Facebook. Loads of girls in particular found my blog and found it to be quite inspiring. Prior to that they also had been unable to find anything that would give them inspiration or encouragement. As a consequence, we built up quite a community of both tattoo collectors and people who were nervous about getting their first tattoo.

How did you select your magazine's name?
My initial prototype was called *Th!ink* and I used that name for my blog as well. But with the word *Th!ink* I don't really feel that you get the full impact of what I'm trying to say and I always felt like it needed explaining. I knew I wanted something that was much simpler for the magazine so I chose *Things & Ink* because it's about the lifestyle as well as the tattoos.

How did you initially fund your magazine?
Through savings.

Really? So you were saving while you were writing for these other magazines?
Yes, every penny of it. For my first issue I printed two thousand copies, which cost me three thousand pounds—all of that came out of my savings.

Who does all your design and photography?
Things & Ink has turned into more of a collaborative project. We have freelance photographers, designers, and writers. I feel that *Things & Ink* gives people the space and the freedom to be creative. For instance, if we do a photo shoot, we'll all pitch in and throw ideas around. As it's a really low budget—or should I say, no budget—magazine [laughs], I don't want to go to people with really strong ideas of how I want things done, because at the end of the day they're not getting paid for it, so I look at it as more of a collaboration where people get the experience and an opportunity to build on their portfolios. I like to give the freedom that they wouldn't necessarily get with another publication and it just seems to work for me.

Although you said there was a gap in the market at the time, how are you different from the competition? Have more people entered that market or do you find that you are still quite niche?

Yes, we are still very niche. I don't think the other tattoo magazines are doing what we do because I regard *Things & Ink* as a coffee table art book—the other magazines seem a little bit more throwaway. *Things & Ink* is published quarterly, it's bigger, and a bit more in-depth, whereas the other magazines are monthly and a little more newsy in style. We've recently changed our identity because originally our tagline read, "Embracing female tattoo culture" because it gave us the edge by mainly focusing on women, but as we've grown I've noticed that we've also picked up a lot of male readers and I felt that it was important for me to recognize that it's not just for women anymore.

About what percentage male to female is your readership and what does your audience look like?

It's about fifty-fifty men and women. Readership ranges from age twenty to about thirty-five. It's made up of people who are tattoo collectors, art lovers, and those who just want more of an intellectual approach to the tattoo lifestyle. They want something that's more in-depth as opposed to just pretty pictures.

Was your blog following very supportive when you launched *Things & Ink*?

Yes.

Did you let them know about the magazine as the launch got closer?

Yes, I blogged the whole journey. Launching the first issue was one of the most difficult things I have ever done in my life—ever! I had absolutely no idea what I was doing. Even though I worked in the magazine world, I still didn't really know how to start a magazine from scratch. It was so difficult—collating all the content and finding designers who could bring my vision to life was also very difficult.

So you had your vision but it was just a matter of communicating it and finding people who could help you bring it to life?

Exactly.

Did you have any ads in that first issue?

I think I might have had one [laughs].

Were you literally just ringing companies up?

No, I still struggle with ads today. Ads are the big thing that's missing from *Things & Ink* because I am just not a salesperson. I have an editorial background and as a consequence I find it quite difficult to make the magazine into a moneymaking business. I think that ad sales require a specific skill, which unfortunately I don't have. I've tried and have slowly built up relationships with companies that I feel sit well with the brand. Now that we've been on the market for quite some time, people are beginning to recognize us as a trusted publication, but getting ads at the very beginning was very difficult.

"A Curious Purity"

"I MET A LADY IN THE MEADS,
FULL BEAUTIFUL, A FAERY'S CHILD;
HER HAIR WAS LONG, HER FOOT WAS LIGHT,
AND HER EYES WERE WILD."

– FROM LA BELLE DAME SANS MERCI
BY JOHN KEATS

Art Director - Marina De Salis
Photographer - Philip Rhys Matthews
Makeup, Hair & Styling - Adrianna Veal
Model - Elena Wood

Makeup: Illamasqua
Nails: Chanel - 38 Rouge Flamboyant
Dolce & Gabbana - Vinaccia
Accessories: Stylist's own

What about distribution, how did you handle that at the time? Were you just packaging up and shipping the copies out yourself?
Yes I was. Distribution is also something I find to be quite difficult because to get into a place like WHSmith you have to pay a listing fee, which most small magazines can't afford, so as a result we are not available in there.

How much is the listing fee?
It's anywhere between one thousand and ten thousand pounds.

Is that per issue or per year?
I had a meeting with a distribution company about it, so I think it's either per quarter or per issue. It makes it very difficult for a low-budget magazine because you pay your listing fee, then it's sale or return, and WHSmith will take around 40 percent anyway, then distribution will take their cut, so by the time the money comes back to you, you're lucky if you make two pounds [laughs].

Where is the magazine distributed now?
Due to the fact that most of our orders come from online, we're now using a company called Newsstand (newsstand.co.uk).

That's probably where I found you, actually.
Probably, yes. They don't take any sums of money up front, they only take £1.75 per copy from the issue and post them out for us as well. It's helped us increase visibility tremendously. Back when the first issue went on sale I had all the magazines at my house. We got two hundred orders on that first day and I panicked straightaway, I was like, "How am I going to go to the post office with two hundred magazines?"—it just wasn't feasible. As soon as that happened I knew I needed to find an alternative because I couldn't run the magazine and go to the post office every single day, which would've been absolutely ridiculous.

And that's when you engaged Newsstand. Are you the only one in-house who's working on the magazine?
Yes, and I still do freelance work as well. I still work for other magazines and newspapers in order to pay the bills.

Briefly describe the process of planning the table of contents to completing the final layout. Where do your ideas come from?
Like I said, it's more of a collaboration, so I have many different contributors who all do different, specific things.

Do you have a set of writers that you use all the time—how does that work?
Yes, we have regular contributors—their names are listed in the masthead. When you look at the masthead of the magazine it looks like there's a massive in-house team, but really all those people have other full-time jobs and so they just contribute their individual parts.

With the TOC, does everyone just pitch their ideas and you see what you like?

Normally I'll come up with the themes, but we also get different ideas when we actually do the photo shoots. For instance, with the illustration issue we thought of the concept for the cover before we decided that that would be the theme. We decided that we'd like an artist to create the artwork and morph it in with a photo of themselves, and so the issue just grew from that single idea. Sometimes we think of the theme first and then the photos and content will come after, or we'll think of an idea for the photo shoot and then decide what the issue should be called.

So it's really an organic process.
Yes, completely.

What do you find the most challenging part of running a magazine literally by yourself?
Definitely the business side. Also, from the outside we look like a highly successful magazine. We look like we've made it, we look like we're a business. The magazine looks really professional, but when you get below the surface it's really hard because we're not making any money—I mean, I'm still doing other freelance work just to support myself. The magazine is a pure labor of love and it's kind of difficult for me when people say, "It looks like it's so successful," when I really know that behind the scenes I am working my butt off to make it happen.

Putting your heart and soul into it…
Yes, for very little monetary reward.

For now! So that's the most challenging but what do you find the most rewarding? What makes you feel good, why do you keep doing this labor of love?
[Laughs] The most rewarding is going from concept to print—it's absolutely awesome seeing it all come together. I really love compiling the issues, thinking of the ideas, doing the shoots, planning it out, I love it. I know there is a massive need for it too. I love when we go and sell the magazine at conventions and someone comes up and says, "I love your magazine, it really speaks to me." That means so much to me—it's amazing.

Now that you've been in the publishing world for a reasonable length of time, what factors do you think contribute to the success of a magazine in general?
It depends what you mean by success really.

That's true. Well, what's your definition of success for a magazine?
I was hoping by now that the success of my magazine would be me in an office with a couple of other people working full-time, but that hasn't happened yet.

Well, you could define success as getting an issue together and putting it out there.
You're right, and yes, that is a success. Two thousand people buy the magazine every issue and that's a small success as well. We've got a small but really captive audience and that's a huge thing. I guess a magazine can have

hundreds of thousands of readers, but ours are very special, they are all collectors of it, they love it, they speak to us, they talk to us, they read...actually, they devour every issue, and I guess that's what's important.

Now we could come back to a definition for failure, for lack of a better word, but if success is that you have an engaged audience, then I guess failure could be having a message that nobody is interested in?
Exactly.

You already said that you are not currently profitable. How soon do you expect to see a profit?
I am thinking as early as next year. While freelancing at a newspaper not too long ago, I met a young man who sells ads and who is willing to sell ads for us on a commission-only basis. He's going to work on the magazine full-time and is very confident about what he can do for me with the ads. I really don't see any reason why certain companies wouldn't want to buy into the *Things & Ink* brand knowing the niche audience that we serve.

Do you set a budget for each issue?
I just spend as little money as possible.

Do you have a set number for your print run?
Yes.

Do you have a predetermined number of pages for each issue?

Yes, it's normally between ninety-six and one hundred pages long.

Are there any other activities that you do or partake in as it relates to the magazine?
Actually, I've curated quite a few exhibitions because tattoos happen to be a very good tie-in for exhibitions. To celebrate our second anniversary I recently curated an exhibition at Atomica Gallery in Covent Garden. We had about one hundred and fifty tattoo artists involved and asked each one to donate a postcard-size work of art with all the proceeds going to charity. It was amazing! We got press coverage from both the *Guardian* and *Metro* newspapers. On the opening night there were so many people lining up outside to get in. That is something I definitely want to do more of, curating exhibitions. I think it really gets people talking and it's also a nice way for me to meet people one-on-one. I also curated an exhibition earlier this year at a tattoo shop, and thinking back, I actually held one for our first year anniversary at Atomica. Exhibitions are a big part of the whole picture and I plan to do a lot more of them next year.

What sorts of skills would you say are important for a magazine publisher to have?
You have to be able to do many different things because you literally have to do everything. You have to understand the business side, you have to be able to write, you have to be able to organize contributors, you have to be able to market, do social media, InDesign—the works.

Do you feel that having a publishing degree has helped you in any way?

No, not really as it was so long ago. I feel that the experience I gained in the magazine world as a writer is what truly helped me. I learned exactly how to put together an issue of a magazine. Like organizing the flatplan, I wouldn't have known what a flatplan was any other way.

Can you explain what it is?

Yes, a flatplan is literally the plan of the magazine—so from page one to say, ninety-six, all the pages are laid out in front of you and you can figure out exactly where everything goes.

Is that hand drawn or is there a particular software that you use to produce it?

I'm sure that some publishers use a fancy software but I literally just create the template in InDesign and draw little squares to represent each page. Then I number them from one to ninety-six and simply decide what goes where and how many pages something should have.

So it's literally like a storyboard, but for a magazine instead of a movie?

Exactly. Then you decide how many pages you want for ads and so forth. So yes, I think my magazine experience was really important, it helped me understand the workflow of how to put an issue together.

Okay, what last message of wisdom or inspiration do you have for somebody who is thinking about starting their own magazine?

I would say don't do it unless you're willing to never sleep again [laughs]. You have to work really hard and you have to truly love what you're doing. Don't launch a magazine to make money, launch it because there is a gap in the market. Launch it because you love what your magazine is going to be about. You have to truly be engaged with the content, you have to really put love into everything you do. Don't just do it to be a moneymaking venture because there's a good chance that it just might not be.

3
x
3

14

3X3

14

CHARLES HIVELY

Magazine name: *3x3*
Founder and publisher: Charles Hively
Year founded: 2003
Tagline: The magazine of contemporary illustration
Editorial mission: To preserve, protect, and promote illustration in all its forms
Location: New York, USA
Website: 3x3mag.com
Formats: Print and digital (PDF format)
Issues per year: Two
Language: English
Reach: Worldwide
Available: Website and newsstands
Circulation: 3,300
Price per issue: $15 USD
One-year subscription: $54 USD
Size of in-house team: Two full-time

Lorraine: Hey there Charles, what were you doing before you decided to start a magazine?
Charles: I was the vice president and creative director for an advertising agency based here in New York.

Where did the idea to produce a magazine come from?
Well, 9/11 happened and the advertising business here in New York just dried up. At the time I made contact with *Graphis* magazine and ended up being the co-publisher along with Marty Pedersen. I was there for about eleven months before I got the idea to create a publication about illustration.

Did you do any market research prior to launching? Did you create some type of business plan or anything like that?
No, not a business plan per se, but I did make some observations. At *Graphis* their annuals included annual reports, advertising, graphic design, photography, new talent, and those types of subjects, but they never did anything on illustration. I asked Marty why that was and he said that nobody would buy it, so he had never even considered it. I kept pressing him because I felt there was a market for illustration, and to test my theory we created an advertising section in the back of the magazine that was used to exclusively advertise photographers in one issue and then exclusively advertise illustrators in the next. He really resisted and was not too happy with any of the illustrators I had selected, but it got me all excited about illustration again, especially since I'd originally started out as an illustrator back in Texas before moving into design and later into advertising. Seeing the work of those illustrators inspired me to put together a sixteen-page dummy magazine.

I had previously been down to Barnes and Noble and found that there was only one other

publication that was actually called *Illustration*, which basically discussed illustration from the '20s and '30s but didn't cover anything that was current or contemporary.

I ended up sending my sixteen-page dummy to the illustrators I had previously selected to advertise in *Graphis* and the reaction I received was overwhelmingly positive. Gary Baseman said that it would never make any money and would end up being a labor of love and Seymour Chwast, from Push Pin Studios fame, didn't think there would be enough support for it. Gary Baseman turned out to be right, but that's another story. Seymour Chwast, however, came to me a year later and said, "I was totally wrong about this," and we ended up moving forward from there—I left *Graphis* to start the magazine.

Interesting.
So yes, there was no plan, but the way I supported the publication was that in the back, similar to what I had done at *Graphis,* I created an advertising section. It didn't consist of any "regular" ads as you would expect to see in a magazine, but each one consisted of a single image along with the contact information for that particular illustrator. Illustrators paid for the space in both the gallery section, which was a single page, and the showcase section, which consisted of a double page spread. I would invite various illustrators to advertise in the publication, and that's how we supported it. The showcase section was for newer illustrators while the gallery was for more established, well-known artists.

So you had advertising from the beginning?
Yes, although as I said, it did not look like advertising at all.

Knowing what you know now, how important do you think it is to start with a plan? Was it more important to do what you did, just create a dummy and get feedback, or should there be some type of written plan as well?
I don't think any of us creatives really do written plans [laughs].

[Laughs] Fair enough.
I think we just basically go and jump, and if it's a success it's a success and if it's a failure, it's a failure. I think a national publication coming out under Condé Nast, for instance, is going to create an in-depth plan. They're going to do the market research, conduct focus group sessions, display cover designs, and so on to the market in order to gauge interest. But in our case, we were not going to be any competition because the publications out there were just not like us.

We did get feedback from the illustrators that we felt would support it, and they did. So in that sense the plan just kind of came together. The first issue and each subsequent issue after that was always a trial. We never knew if we were going to get an issue published or not because we had to have the ads first in order to pay for printing, the major cost for any publication.

In addition to that, I felt like I didn't want to do any competitions. If you look at organizations like *Communication Arts* or *American Illustration*, they all do some type of show and I didn't want to conduct any myself. But I had a board of advisors who I'd constantly bounce ideas off and one of my questions to them was, "Do you think I should do a show?" to which they replied, "Yes, definitely, you need to do a show." So holding functions like those help to fund the operation as well as raise awareness about the magazine.

Where did the name *3x3* come from? Is it "three times three" or "three by three"?
It's actually "three by three" but "three times three" works as well. It's published three times a year, and features three illustrators in each issue, so that's where it came from. But it was a moment of serendipity that happened because my daughter was living in New York at the time and I was going to meet her at Grand Central Terminal. I got on at 33rd Street and when I looked at the three and the three of 33rd I really liked the way they looked together—I was like, "Yeah, three times three and I have three illustrators three times a year—that makes sense." And that's exactly how it happened, it was just like that. I didn't have any idea of a name for the magazine when I got on that train but I certainly had one by the time I got off.

How did you initially fund the magazine? You said that ads were purchased by illustrators, was that basically it?
Yes, that was it. There was no money put into it at all. Don't forget that this was a really rough time in New York, the start of the recession. There wasn't a lot of business and to get those sixteen illustrators to lay down almost a thousand dollars to buy a space in a magazine they'd never seen was quite supportive, but because of this structure we never knew whether the magazine would last for one issue, three, or what.

Steven Heller recently published a book titled *100 Classic Graphic Design Journals*, which showcases the hundred most influential design publications of all time, and I'm proud to say that we're among those listed. But what's so interesting when you read the book is that there are publications that didn't make but three issues, there are publications that only lasted a year, so it's not uncommon for a magazine in this particular category to not make it.

What contributing factors do you think have allowed you to last this long?
Well number one, I think, is that we had continual support from the industry. They understood that this was a startup; they understood that they were going to be an integral part of the magazine and I made it pretty clear that without their support there wouldn't be an issue.

When I look back on it now, I would get comments like, "This is almost like a fundraiser." My editorials would say get involved, help support the effort, and those types of things, and it was

Cat MacInnes. *View more of Cat's work at www.catmacinnes.com or contact her at info@catmacinnes.com, + 61 418 354 439.*

working pretty well until the recession hit. At the time I just couldn't get the per-page cost that I needed to help produce the magazine so I would say to the illustrators, "Let me know how much you can afford this time around."

I feel that illustrators don't spend enough money promoting themselves in general, and I feel that they really need to spend much more but they don't. I knew it was a sacrifice for them to spend money during those tough times, and that slowed our progress down considerably.

The recession also hurt newsstand sales. I think we saw two-thirds of our sales in the UK just drop off when Borders went bankrupt, and then after that US Borders went bankrupt so we lost some more, and then the internet started to take over, so now our audience could go online to research illustrators, making it a totally different environment than when we had started out in 2003. I do think that 2003 was a perfect time, but it probably would have been even better had I started a little earlier like in 1999 or 2000 because it would have given us a little more ramp-up time.

So your initial vision for the magazine was to expose illustrators?
Yes, to a market that I didn't feel was fully respecting illustration at the time. When I got to New York, if you asked an art director whether they used illustration, the answer would usually be no and if you asked them why, most would say, "Because nobody uses illustration. It's dead." To most of them Norman Rockwell was the last famous illustrator, so they weren't really up on the new, young, talented illustrators.

Has your vision changed any over the past ten years?
No, the vision is still there. Actually it's a bit like a pendulum that swings one way and then back the other, and what I started to see in 2004 was that it was unfortunately starting to swing back a little bit. The recession just slowed everything down, the top illustrators were still working and getting assignments, but the second and third tier of illustrators almost vanished from the face of the earth. It was really sad when that happened and that really slowed our momentum. I mean, the momentum had started but that recession almost stopped it altogether. I do have to say that the economy is starting to pick up now and what I am seeing is a lot more use of illustration again. I'm also noticing the rise of a lot of new faces that I haven't seen or heard of before.

Who is the magazine aimed at and what does your audience look like?
Our audience is primarily made up of illustrators, graphic designers, art directors, educators, and students. Initially we didn't go after art buyers but decided to in later years.

How did you initially attract your readers? I don't think social media was around then, but email, flyers, or a launch party, etc.?

No launch party—an email blast was primarily what we did. In the early days I had a list that I would copy ten names from, stick them into an email, and then send them all out as blind copies. We didn't have the system in place like we do now with a database of about fourteen thousand names or so. Back then it was really bare bones and an extremely manual process.

How did you create that first list? Where did those addresses come from?

Well I started out with the sixteen illustrators that I had sent the comp to and then I branched out from there. I was like, "Okay we've got that sixteen so let's find another," as they were my primary target as far as getting the magazine printed, and once it was printed I could promote it from there. The Association of Illustrators in London, AOI, was also very helpful with getting the word out in the UK.

What were your steps in achieving worldwide distribution for *3x3*?

I went to Barnes and Noble and looked at, number one, who was printing some of the publications and, number two, who was distributing them, as you can usually find that information in the masthead or the back of the book somewhere. I found that Central Books in London was a big distributor for Europe, Ingram was big here in the States, and Disticor big in Canada, so I just approached them all.

I had sample copies of the first issue, which was the real killer because you actually had to have something published before you could get a distributor to even take a look, and as a result there were hardly any sales of the first issue because it simply wasn't visible. If I was going to do a publication today, and for instance had four distributors I wanted to approach, I would go to a print-on-demand company like Blurb and do a short run on the first issue. Yeah, it would cost me about thirty bucks a pop but then I wouldn't have to print two thousand of them in order to get a distributor excited about it. But once the distributors saw that first issue they got pretty excited about it because it was such a unique publication. However, I do think it was a bit of a leap of faith on their part for them to actually take us on.

So you were able to get distribution for the second issue because you used the first to showcase your magazine?

Yeah. They usually ask for three copies, so you send along three copies, which they look through and do a show-and-tell with their sales force to see how many issues they think they can sell at what locations or regions, then they place a print order based on that.

How many of you do you actually have working in-house?

Two, my business partner Sarah Munt and me.

I was going to ask what their titles were but… [laughs]

[Laughs] Yes, it's just the two of us. We've had interns over the years and we still have a freelance intern that comes in two or three days a week but it's primarily the two of us that put out the magazine. *Creative Quarterly*, our other magazine, comes out four times a year and then there's the *3x3 Illustration Annual* and the *3x3 Illustration Directory*.

The directory was a result of us again trying to encourage art directors to use illustration, so it's sent out every year for free to six thousand art directors and art buyers in the US alone. We send it for free because we know they wouldn't pay for it, but it's a way for us to get that market excited about illustration. Sometimes they'll even become subscribers of the magazine, but that's not what the purpose is as the purpose is to have them see and hire the illustrators.

I take it that you also use freelancers.
Yes, we use freelance photographers but not freelance writers. With *3x3* what we do is have fellow illustrators write an article about an illustrator. So we'll approach an illustrator and say, "Who would you like to have write this article on you?" and they'll obviously pick someone who knows them pretty well.

I really thought that was the way to go about it, because then the illustrator who writes the story would also get a free page in the gallery section or the showcase section and that's how they'd be paid. We use freelance photographers to take pictures of people's studios, which is another important feature of the magazine. Most times the illustrator will recommend somebody to us and we'll just contact them to do the photography.

With two issues out a year, how long does it typically take you to put an issue together?
Well…it takes a long time. In the beginning we were getting three issues out, but as soon as we introduced the annual, that slowed everything down considerably because the annual is a pretty good size, it's around three to four hundred pages. So what we were able to do for the most part was two issues of the ninety-six-page magazine and one of the annual.

Would you briefly describe the process from planning the table of contents to completing of the final layout?
Yes. Well, the first job is to select the illustrators. What I like to do is select three that I feel will work well together in the publication. So I'm looking for diversity of style as well as diversity of location, I like to get as many international illustrators as possible. I then approach them to see if they're interested and most times they are. I think I've only had one person turn me down and that was because they didn't want a photographer coming into their studio [laughs]. They didn't want any strangers in their studio—I guess I can kind of understand that.

So yes, we select the three and I send them a list of twenty questions that we ask of every illustrator. I then ask for a lead on who's going to write the story and send that lead copies of previous articles so they can become familiar with our style. I require that the stories be returned in essay format, and once that's done then I'll send a shot list to the photographer. There's usually a two-month lead for all that to happen, so let's say that if it's in October, then by December 1 we would want to have everything complete. In the meantime I'm selling ads, inviting people to be featured in the gallery or showcase sections, and that takes up a lot of my time as well.

You do the ad sales yourself?

Yes, and pack the magazines and send them out too, so yes, I'm a jack-of-all-trades. And there are always delays. If you're asking an illustrator to write a story, it's not like hiring a copywriter who'd do it in three weeks and turn it in perfectly edited, revisions and all. With an illustrator—or basically anybody that's not a copywriter—sometimes there'll be grammatical and spelling errors, so it's necessary to do internal fixes that we may have an intern on the outside handle. But I do have to say that I've been very impressed by the writing skills of the illustrators. So it could take four months to get one issue even started, but once it starts it's pretty quick from there, I would say within two to three weeks we would have the thing ready to go to press—so that would make it about five months for each issue.

What do you find the most challenging about running a magazine?

I think it's that there are just so many parts to it. What you're hoping for is that your readers subscribe because it's financially beneficial for you. When you send the magazines to a distributor you have to discount it 55 percent leaving you 45 percent of the cover price, but then you're responsible for paying the shipping costs to them, so the actual income you get back is very low, especially at the beginning. So you're hoping for a good number of subscribers, a good number of newsstand sales, and the support of the community through advertising, etc. There are so many different variables that have to run almost perfectly in sync.

What do you find the most rewarding then? What makes you feel good as far as working on the publication?

I think when somebody tells you that they read the magazine cover to cover—that's what we're looking for. Also when we get good feedback, because we are really good about doing readership surveys. We do a number of other surveys, like income surveys to find out what illustrators are making all over the world, which nobody else had ever done. So the feedback we would get—which was very surprising to me because I'm thinking the visuals are the most important part of this—was that they wanted more text, they wanted more in-depth articles. So we actually expanded the text with the amount of words going from around seven hundred to a thousand or more because we knew that's what our readers wanted. So yes, the most satisfying part is to see that people like what we're doing and understand why we're doing it.

KAREN BARBOUR. *Karen is a published author and an illustrator of children's books and young adult books. Her dramatic, vibrant paintings combine folk art and magic realism and have been recognized by the American Institute of Graphic Arts, American Illustration, Society of Illustrators and multiple Parent's Choice Awards. Trained as a fine artist, Karen exhibits regularly in Los Angeles, San Francisco, Rome, Milan, Tokyo, New York and most recently had a show in Abano, Italy. Her commissioned work includes recent* The New York Times Op-Ed *pages as well as work for* Newsweek, Vogue, Harpers, Rolling Stone, *Harper Collins, Scholastic, Ralph Lauren and Estée Lauder. View more of Karen's work at www.karenbarbour.com or contact her at kbarbour@svn.net, 415 259 8667.*

Have you ever felt like giving up?
Oh, sure.

And why didn't you?
I think...well the short answer to that is I think I did give up [laughs].

[Laughs] Well you're still publishing, so maybe not.
Let me explain. Back in 2014 we made a conscious decision to no longer publish the magazine because it seemed like we were just not getting enough subscribers. Subscriptions had basically dropped off. With the recession, it was not a flat thing, it was just a continuous spiral down. Newsstand sales were dropping off as well, which meant that distributors were ordering less. The annual, on the other hand, was just skyrocketing. If we did three thousand copies of the magazine as a request for print, we'd do five to seven thousand copies of the annual, so it was a no-brainer. If you're spending all your time, you know, ten months out of the year, trying to get two issues out with subscriptions and distribution dropping off, but the annual sales were hot and people were buying them either at the newsstand or online, it would be more prudent for us to figure out the annual should be what we're putting most of our energy into. And we've used this year to plan what we want to do in 2015 in addition to the annual.

So it's not necessarily giving up then, it's more like switching gears?

Yes. The mission is still the same. I don't think that the mission has changed, but what I'm trying to do now is to create a series of monographs featuring a single illustrator with more pages because the magazine is about ninety-six pages and I want to increase that to one hundred and twenty-eight or more with no advertising to speak of. We will offer single and subscription opportunities. You would subscribe to two to three monographs a year which will be much easier for me because there won't be ad sales that I have to deal with, which took up a lot of my time. So we're going to try that and see how it works. Also, we've started offering digital issues of all the back issues of *3x3* and there are still a limited number of print editions available too.

Can you explain what a monograph is?
Certainly, if you go to a bookstore your favorite artist will usually have a monograph. Monograph, meaning one person that's featured in a book, so that's what we're going to do. I'm selecting three illustrators—just as I did with the magazine—who don't overlap and are really totally unique. I'm inviting them to participate, doing pretty much the same thing with the photography, getting that assigned, getting the preface and the forward assigned to other illustrators or industry leaders, and then I will use the directory pages for payment for those contributors. So it's kind of the same thing, but you're right, it's more of a shift away from a magazine to more of a regularly published book.

Charles, previously you stated that the market has changed and there are now fewer subscriptions coming in and you're seeing more of a downward spiral as opposed to it being either flat or on the increase. Do you have any answers as to why that may be? Is this just for your particular niche?

Well, I think the internet had a huge impact. I think that when Facebook came around illustrators were able to share their art with their friends, so to speak.

Yes, because now you have websites like Behance, deviantART, and Dribbble.

Exactly, and then you've got Instagram and Twitter—you've also got Tumblr. A lot of those sites were nonexistent in 2003. I don't think that those types of sites can truly support an effort because they're so "piecemeal." I think that when you go on—and I go on two or three times a day—there's nothing that you can actually see and hold.

I have to say that about five years ago you were seeing a real trend of wanting things digitally, and so we started offering digital subscriptions. That went on for a while and then it almost turned backwards, and what I was hearing was, "Oh no, if you just have it in digital I don't want it. I want it in print. I want something I can hold." And again, that's part of our mission. When you look back a hundred years from now I want what we have produced to be a guidepost as to what was happening in the industry worldwide, and I think that's another reason

that the monographs will help because once again, it's establishing illustration as something that's very important as an art form.

What factors do you feel can contribute to the success of a magazine?

I think niche publications have a much better chance of success. When you look on the newsstand, let's just take food and wine as a category, there's a bunch of them, there's a bunch of lifestyle magazines, but you probably only need one or two. I mean when you get past the two, what's the third one going to look like? It's got to be unique enough and different enough for it to really have any draw, otherwise I'm going to stick with the publications I know whether it's *Bon Appétit*, *Martha Stewart Living*, or whatever it may happen to be. Although it can be done, to get another publication in that category I think would be very difficult. It takes a lot of marketing and a lot of planning in finding a way to make it unique and different.

At one point during the recession I was looking online and there were four hundred and twenty-five magazines going out business every year with only twenty of those coming back in as a new publication. I think that demonstrated how particular categories had way too many publications.

What do you think contributes to a magazine's failure, is it being in a category (or segment) that's oversaturated?

Yeah, I don't think there was a need for all those publications. There wasn't enough support on the newsstand or coming in from subscriptions. Major publications like *Martha Stewart Living* and *Bon Appétit* literally give their subscriptions away since they make most of their money from the advertising and they can get that support. A company like Condé Nast can just say, "You know, I'll give you two pages in this publication if you put one page in our new publication," or that type of thing. So they're able to move advertising dollars in, but that can only last so long because the public has to actually go out and buy the magazine or start subscribing at some point.

Is it fair to say that, due to some of the things we've already discussed, *3x3* is not profitable at this time?
Yes, and actually we've never been profitable.

So it's always been a break-even type deal?
Exactly.

In that case how did you go about setting a budget for the magazine?
Well, you pretty much know what you need to spend as far as printing. And since we're also a design firm, the design time was a giveaway. When I go speak to student groups I tell them that we're not a publisher in the true sense of the word since a publisher would have a design department or simply freelance that out. But we're basically a design firm that publishes art and design magazines and books. It's a totally different scenario. If we had to charge for design time we'd never have published anything—we really wouldn't—we just couldn't have afforded to.

So your major revenue stream comes from the other sources that you've mentioned?
Yes. The directory we give away, but the annual is our major revenue stream. The annual is the result of entries that are submitted for consideration and then juried for exhibition in the book. And just to clarify, when I say we've never been profitable, yes, we've made money, but that's not adding in any of the design time, because if I added that in then we might go broke [laughs].

What do you foresee for the magazine publishing industry in general?
I think that it's rebounding, I really do. I think there's an increased need for something that's printed. It went away for a while but I perceive that it's coming back. Again, I think that to be successful you have to be in a niche that fewer people are in.

Are you seeing less value in digital now?
Yes.

Why do you think that is?
I think because—well a perfect example is me. I used to subscribe to a bunch of magazines, *Print* magazine in particular was one that I used to subscribe to. I stopped subscribing to *Print* last year and switched to the digital

subscription instead. I ended up receiving six issues but I've only looked at one. I think I'm just not that involved with it because it's not right in front of me where I can simply grab it. I bought the subscription because I still wanted to keep in touch and it was cheaper to do it that way; plus I didn't need any more magazines stacking up—as you know in New York we don't have a lot of space anyway. But I think that's what happens to magazines that you get in digital if you've had them in print before.

Now when my partner got her iPad I did say, "No way, I won't do that," but I look at *Martha Stewart Living* and *ELLE DECOR* because I really love the images on the tablet—they are just as good and strong as what shows on my screen, whereas you'd have that loss with print.

But there again I feel that the pendulum swung all the way over to digital and now it's slowly coming back. I mean you spend so much time in front of a screen, after you quit work and have ended for the day do you really want to go home and look at another screen? Especially looking at things on the iPhone—I think it's absolutely ridiculous to look at a magazine on an iPhone [laughs] but there are people who do. The tablet I can understand and appreciate, but you can only put so many publications on an iPad, I'm already having to archive because I'm running out of space.

I think there are a number of reasons that print will continue to be an important medium. The general public is seeing way too much on a screen, and what's the alternative to that? It's a print publication.

What types of skills do you consider necessary for a magazine publisher to have today?
That's a very interesting question because our printer on *Creative Quarterly* is currently doing an issue about that. I think the design, especially if you look at trade publications in particular—they are really ugly. It's poor photography, poor layout, poor typography, poor use of illustration, poor cover design—I mean there are so many bad things going on. They're really not interested in making a good publication—it's for their trade organization so it's almost like a glorified newsletter.

I think publishers really need to care about how their magazines are packaged, what size it is, how the photography and illustration looks and is used. They should really try to create an interesting package, because ultimately that's what people gravitate towards. It's no different from, let's say, a package in a grocery store—you're going to be drawn to that package for some reason, maybe the label appears interesting to you. That happens a lot with wines, you have no idea what that wine tastes like but because you really like the packaging you buy it, and I don't think it's any different with a publication on the shelf because something has to draw you in. That's certainly the purpose of the cover, to draw you in, make you pick it up and hopefully have a thumb-through, and then make a purchase if the content inside is equal to what you originally appreciated on the cover.

What last message of wisdom would you like to leave with someone who might be considering starting a publication of their own?
Well, the advice that I got I think was pretty true. If you're an independent entity that wants to put out a magazine, then you have to do it as a labor of love first. Don't count on it being successful. Don't count on making any money from it. And if you're still saying, "Okay, let's do it," then I think you've invested yourself in it.

If you say, "Oh, I have this idea for a magazine, let's do it," I don't think that will be as successful as if you put your whole heart and soul into it, if you give it 110 percent. You can do all the marketing and business plans in the world but if you are not personally invested, then you'd better do it for a reason other than the money.

Finally, is there anything else you'd like to add or wish I had asked?
Well, I think your question about revenue streams is interesting, because I think that you have to figure that out. I have some ideas for publications where revenue would be generated from advertising sales, but then you have to find someone who's going to sell those ads for you. It's a magazine that's kind of built around the same premise as *3x3*, but it's an investment of time to find that person to go out and sell the ads, and then how do you pay that person and all of those kinds of things. I think those types of issues are important for a publication that has to be solely funded by ad sales, and I think that's a big "if" when you're looking at a publication, because that's the way you're going to support the people that have to produce it, design it, write for it—all of those things that you have to have in place in order to run as a "normal" publication.

So advertising sales are key, but you have to reach the threshold of around ten thousand copies before you can start attracting major advertisers like Adobe Creative Cloud to actually advertise. With most of the publications I've seen—and this was also verified by what Heller did—you're talking about three to four thousand in circulation. It was never up into the five-digit numbers which is what you really need in order to support a publication with true advertising. You can do pro bono ads or barter for something, but you have to get to that number in circulation and that's hard as hell to do—for a niche magazine anyway.

vna

CONOR HARRINGTON

MODE 2 / SHAWN BARBER / SHOE
RONZO / REM ROUGH

Very Nearly Almost 18   £5.00

VERY NEARLY ALMOST (VNA)

GEORGE MACDONALD

Magazine name: *Very Nearly Almost* (*VNA*)
Founder and editor: George Macdonald
Year founded: 2006
Tagline: Art culture
Editorial mission: Documenting the fastest-growing art movement in the last one hundred years
Location: London, UK
Website: verynearlyalmost.com
Formats: Print, blog, clothing, and stickers
Issues per year: Four
Language: English
Reach: Worldwide
Available: Website, digital newsstands, newsstands, bookstores, and independent stores
Circulation: 8,000
Price per issue: £5.99 (approx. $9.04 USD)
One-year subscription: £20 (approx. $30.18 USD)
Size of in-house team: Six part-time

Lorraine: George, tell me what you did before you launched your magazine.

George: Well, I've always been involved in design and photography. I did my degree in photography and ended up working for photographers and various magazines doing jobs like picture editing. I was unable to get a full-time job anywhere so ended up working on a design project with my dad. I had so much spare time that I started taking lots of photographs of street art and in a roundabout way that's how the magazine came about.

Where did your love for graffiti and street art come from?

I've known about graffiti and street art since I was around thirteen or fourteen and was actually involved a little bit in graffiti myself as a kid, although not anything serious. I've always followed graffiti and street art and photographed it. I almost became addicted to it. I just love every bit of it.

What gave you the idea to start a publication about it? Was there anything comparable at the time?

There were other graffiti magazines out there but nothing that talked to street art. Street art was starting to become an art form in itself and I wanted to do something creative, so I thought of starting a zine that I could give away for free. I had no intentions of it becoming a business, I just wanted a creative portal for myself. I had taken so many photographs both on film and on digital that I just didn't know what to do with them all, so I roughly put them together in Photoshop, printed it all up, photocopied them, and passed them out. The reaction I got was so good that I ended up doing it again and again—everything just blew up from there.

Your magazine was founded in 2006—was that for the initial photocopied version or did that mark the launch of the actual magazine as we know it today?

September 2006 was when I started out with the photocopied zines.

So how soon after that did the magazine come about?
Probably about six months.

Really, that quickly?
Yeah. I always put the website address on the back of the magazine and I got so much reaction from it that it started to create a buzz. I'd get tons of contact through email—because there wasn't much social media back then—but the reaction was so good that I just wanted to keep it going.

Did you have a business plan or did you just follow your heart?
There was no plan since it really did happen organically. I know that sounds cheesy, but the plan was not to have a magazine. The plan was just to create some zines and see how far I could take it, see whether people enjoyed them.

The street art scene was really blowing up at the time and I felt that it was strong enough to where I didn't feel the need to think that far ahead, I just wanted to keep riding the wave and keep doing more and more, and lucky for me it worked out. In retrospect now, had I had a business plan I probably would have become an actual business much sooner.

Why did you select *Very Nearly Almost* as the title for your magazine?

The name goes back to me always wanting to do something creative. I had done lots of little things before. I used to own a clothing label that really didn't go anywhere. I thought I could be a DJ, I thought I could be an artist, but none of it went anywhere. It was this whole "very nearly almost" there, nearly making it but not quite. I think I had too many fingers in too many pies. I was always in pursuit of exciting creative ideas but not really giving each one the focus, dedication, and concentration it required, so it was always "very nearly almost" for me and that's where the name comes from.

How did you initially fund the magazine? I can't imagine going from free photocopies to a slick magazine.
I never really invested any money in it. The first two issues were photocopied for free as I just printed them at work, and then the third issue was printed by some guys out of Germany called Cromatics who emailed me and said "We'd like to print *VNA*," so they did, and at a very reasonable price.

How many copies did you print with them?
A thousand copies. I think we were at about thirty-two pages back then but it was mostly printed in black and white. By the time I sold a few online, I made my money back and that gave me enough to invest in the next print run, which I then did in color. Any money I made I would just invest it back, and it kept on going like that. I never really invested any money in it at all except for the first website and a small

amount of start-up money, which is why I say it just organically grew from there. I would have to say that it was more luck than judgment.

How were you selling the magazines initially?
I had a very crude website at the time, but there was an online forum called the Banksy forum where people would go to talk about art, street art, and things of that nature. Through that I was able to contact a lot of people—they loved the magazine and spread the word about it. People just kept buying and I managed to keep riding my luck and keep printing new ones.

Issue three was still black and white but professionally printed. Four and five were printed in color but it was still only thirty-two pages. Then I tried a new printer who gave me a better quality print and more color pages. I just kept stepping it up as I got enough money to keep investing in it.

At issue seven I met Greg Beer who is now our art director . He really loved the magazine and wanted to help me out since he could tell that I wasn't a designer per se. I couldn't do the layout like he could so he decided to take it all on board. He said, "You've got to choose really good paper—you've got to do this, you've got to do that." He made various changes, essentially redoing the entire layout, and in the process he changed what I had into a "real" magazine.

I'm not sure why, but I think most people would associate graffiti with America. Is there anybody else doing what you do and how do you deal with the competition, whether it's print, online, or a topical blog?

There are a few and, yeah, graffiti did start in America but UK has its own scene too. The street art scene, which is a separate thing from graffiti, is big as well.

What's the difference between street art and graffiti?

Traditionally graffiti is just spray paint on walls, whereas street art could include stickers, stencils, posters, 3D sculptures, just anything that's creative and put in the street. That's the way I look at it anyway.

And you're saying that there is competition from other magazines?

Yes. There are lots of creative magazines that touch on street art and graffiti.

So what is your niche?

I would like to think that by now we have established a reputable brand, plus we are constantly trying to find really interesting content, always looking to step up our content by finding interesting people that no one else has featured. And at the end of the day that's all you can really do.

What does your audience look like? What kind of age group? Do you know much about them, hobbies, etc. Are they artists?

I'd like to think that the age range is from maybe sixteen to forty. Not only do we touch on street art but we also touch on illustration, design, and photography—so people who are interested in any of those subjects will hopefully be drawn to the magazine. You could say designers or photographers, but also people who are at college. We've been contacted by a lot of people at college who are trying to find their way artistically, who are really into all the topics that we feature.

How do people find out about your magazine? How important is social media in that whole process?

Social media is massive for us now. It's pretty much how we get our message across for new releases and basically anything to do with the magazine. We use it to contact people for help if we are looking for an artist or if we want to get the readers' input— it's good for those types of things and we do listen to our audience.

Are there any particular channels that work better for you than others?

The interaction happens mostly through Instagram and Facebook and a little bit on Twitter. There are several of us who can handle it, so we all just jump in wherever we can and take it on. I like to think that we have really good communication with our followers.

What about distribution? Are you worldwide?

Yeah. I first got distribution in about 2008 or 2009 and just for a very small amount, I think

it was like five hundred magazines, so it's definitely grown since then. The great thing about it is that the more people see it, read it, or hear about it, the more people that buy it and talk about it—it just keeps spreading, almost generically, like that.

Briefly tell me how you go from planning the TOC to completing the final layout.

Layout is definitely more Greg's side as that's his expertise. We start out quite early and probably have about 60–75 percent of an issue complete when we're about a month away from print. Of course, the last two weeks are manic and everything goes crazy.

I couldn't give you exact timings on the process because every issue is different, plus we don't work on it full-time, we only work on it part-time. So we don't all sit in an office thinking about things—it just happens when we get the time to meet up at our office in Hackney. It's an organic process that somehow seems to work.

What do you find most challenging about running a magazine?

It's hard to answer that one because we do it for the love; we don't really make that much money from it. I think the hardest thing is just the time, trying to spread your time evenly between family, work, and side projects like this *VNA*. That probably is it. And also, you know, the financial struggle to keep it going, to keep finding advertisers. It's quite a lot of work really [laughs].

So what do you find most rewarding?

It's that moment when you hold your magazine in your hand, you know? Still to this day, it's just the best feeling to see all of that work come together when I get it back from the printers—and I love physical print anyway—so to be able to hold your piece of print is just... there is no feeling like it. So yeah, that's probably the biggest reward. To see that people buy it, and the reaction from people on our social media is also pretty incredible as well.

What factors do you think contribute to the success of a magazine?

I think finding a subject that you are most passionate about—that is probably the key—and then just roll with it. I know it's quite easy for me to say, "Oh, just let it grow organically," because it's not that easy for everyone, but for me that's exactly how it worked. I wouldn't put too much pressure on yourself unless you are desperately trying to make a massive living out of it, in which case you really should have a business plan. So yes, having a business plan would also be good advice.

What do you think contributes to the failure of a magazine?

I'd like to think that just changing things up is enough to keep people interested. We started very, very niche as a magazine and that can become a bit tiresome quickly unless you are gaining followers all the time. To keep things interesting we've brought in new creative people to feature, from tattoo artists to fine artists. Just really creative people who we feel have good stories to tell and who we think our audience will enjoy reading about. So I think constantly changing content and perspectives is very important for a niche publication like ours.

What would you say is your secret for running the magazine eight years now? That's definitely something to be admired.

Thank you. Hmm, the secret? I would say surrounding myself with people who are like-minded and who are also in creative industries has really helped. I already mentioned Greg our art director, but we also have a copywriter called Zang who I've known for five years now. He's always helped out since I met him. Roly, our manager, he's now taking on the day-to-day running of the magazine. We've got a video guy called Pete and our web guy is called Ben. He takes care of the website and a lot of our social stuff, plus we have two great writers by the names of Geoff and Gin. So yeah, just really good people who are into the idea of the magazine and are motivated to keep building it up in order to make it successful.

You say you are profitable? How long did it take before you saw a profit?

Well, we're not really profitable but more at breakeven. We did generate a minimal profit last year. Lucky for us it's really not about the money, it's just about continuously pushing our magazine out there. Eventually we would like to have a proper office because we have a shared office at the moment, but if we can keep

going and keep building, the idea would be to have a proper office one day, and who knows what after that.

Are there any additional activities you do that also generate income for the magazine?
Yes. We do collaboration T-shirts with certain artists. We've also done sticker packs, scarves, and different types of things in the past.

What's great about *VNA* is that it's all about interacting with the artists, so we are always on the look out for new people to work with. We like to get really creative people involved who can create great T-shirts that are going to sell well. It's very useful to have those extra income sources because it really helps towards the bottom line.

Where do you sell these items? In the magazine, on your website, or through your social media channels?
On the website and through social media. The word spreads very quickly on social media, so anything you've got new, put it straight up there, and if people like it they'll buy—as long as you're not ripping them off.

So social media is an effective way to sell?
Yeah, it really helps us connect directly with our readers, being a niche magazine it's important for us to not only rely on advertising.

What about advertisers? How do you decide what advertisers go with your particular niche? Do you find them or do they find you?
It's a bit of both really. The more popular you become, the more people notice you and think, "Oh, maybe I'll get involved with their mag." PR companies are always looking for new avenues to bring their brands through. Sometimes there have been big brands that we've loved and really chased. We've emailed them to try and get some level of communication going to see if they're on our wavelength and find out if they're interested. But since our print run isn't huge we still can't demand big numbers, which is always difficult when you're trying to cover print costs.

What skills do you think are important for magazine publishers today?
Skills…I think it really depends on the type of magazine, because with creative magazines obviously you need to have a creative background or knowledge of the field. Also, if you're self-publishing you need to be familiar with professional design tools such as InDesign. I think determination is important as well, oh yeah, and patience too.

Finally, what advice would you have for someone who might be thinking about starting their own publication?
Although it may seem like the obvious answer, you have to have passion for what you're doing and be a bit "ballsy." Even though it's just you sitting on your bed creating the magazine, don't be afraid at the beginning to act a little bigger than what you are, without being silly about it of course, making out like there's a dozen of you in an office somewhere. Just go for it, because as I said, the best thing about it is being able to go through all of the pain, suffering, long sleepless nights, the money worries, and so on—but to hold that magazine in your hands at the end of the day, is just the best feeling in the world.

Wax Poetics
Issue 5

Daft Punk

WAX POETICS

ANDRE TORRES

Magazine name: *Wax Poetics*
Founder and publisher: Andre Torres
Year founded: 2001
Tagline: The best music magazine on the planet
Editorial mission: Exploring the relationship between the past, present, and future music of the black diaspora
Location: Brooklyn, NY
Website: waxpoetics.com
Formats: Print, blog, and digital
Issues per year: Six
Languages: English and Japanese
Reach: Worldwide
Available: Website, digital newsstands, newsstands, specialty shops, and record stores
Circulation: 60,000
Price per issue: $11.99 USD
One-year subscription: US $32.00, Canada $36.00, International $85.00 (all in USD)
Size of in-house team: Three full-time

Lorraine: Hi Andre, what was you up to before you launched your magazine?

Andre: Pretty much everything really. I got my degree in painting and then moved to New York, thinking I was going to get my master's degree. When I first got to New York I worked at the Metropolitan Museum of Art and was completely inundated with people who were pretty much on the same track. I could see that the museum situation had made it very comfortable for a lot of people. They had consequently wasted their time and eight years later were still working as security guards.

At that time I was fumbling around with records and making beats. I eventually got fed up with the whole art thing so I went out and got a corporate job selling software at the World Trade Center. During that time I started to get really antsy to do something creative again and knowing that I didn't want to go all the way into the art world, I initially had an idea to create a documentary, even though I had no prior filmmaking experience. I wanted to tell the story of how record collecting and DJing was an important element of the hip-hop culture.

My research for the documentary led me to realize that there was not much information out there for those like me, who were interested in older music of the African diaspora and its artists, both known and unknown. I realized that if there was ever going to be a documentary made, someone would need to compile the information first, so I wound up making the decision to create a magazine instead of a documentary.

So there wasn't any market research on the magazine per se, but I guess your research for the documentary revealed that there wasn't anything that spoke to your need as far as the information you were looking for at the time.

Yeah, that's it. I mean obviously I'd come up during the age of all the big hip-hop publications like *Source*, *XXL*, and *Ego Trip*.

How are you different from those publications? Do they feature more current hip-hop artists but what you wanted to deal with was more old school?

Yeah, the way I always looked at it was that it was stuck in a vacuum—as if this form of music existed outside of every other form of black music especially. Plus, it was a little more insular and had gotten off a lot more into the lifestyle component of things, whereas my main focus was the music itself. Those magazines really didn't speak to me or to what I was looking for. And after being on the internet in early 2000, I knew there was a growing community, or subculture, of people like me who were searching for records to sample. So I set out to do something that put hip-hop in context by connecting it to all the other music of the black diaspora like soul, reggae, and African music. I wanted to show how all these types of music were indeed a part of the lineage.

How did you come up with your magazine's name, *Wax Poetics*?

We had been fumbling around with the idea of digging in the crates, mainly thinking about vinyl and records. I think the term "wax" spoke to me in regard to the fact that we were talking about so much music that was not available at the time. It's a lot different now with services like Spotify and iTunes, but back then the only way you could find music was by listening to or buying records.

One night I couldn't get to sleep. I got out of bed at about three in the morning and wrote "Wax Poetic" on the wall. I stared at it for a couple of minutes then added the "s" and for some reason it just made sense to me. I went to sleep and the next day I called my partners and said, "I think I have the name of the magazine—*Wax Poetics*."

So it literally came to you during your sleep?

Yeah, or the lack thereof. That kind of spoke to the whole record and vinyl thing and the discussion of music as a sort of play on words, as it got at everything I was trying to say in a kind of poetic manner, so I just ran with it.

How did you initially fund your magazine?

I was laid off from the World Trade Center literally a month before the towers went down, so I had some unemployment money. At that point I had been writing emails to people I'd seen online who I felt had something interesting to say. I had done a lot of sales and recruiting in my office job, so I had adapted this technique to recruiting the writers. I would just email them and say, "Hey, I love this piece that you did. I've got this idea for a magazine and would love you to be a contributor to it."

At the time I had exhausted all my savings and what little I was making on unemployment insurance. Lucky for me, I had two partners

WP

AALIYAH

that had better credit than me. One had some credit card money and the other's father was kind enough to give us a loan of about ten thousand dollars, but after the whole World Trade Center incident I wasn't even sure if we were still going to do it.

By that time I had most of the magazine pretty much together since we had worked on it throughout the year, but I was still unsure because I knew a bunch of people who were actually inside the Towers at the time of the attack, and I couldn't quite see the point of a music magazine at that particular time. After about two weeks, however, I came to the realization that I could've also been in there myself and was truly lucky to even be alive; so I decided that if we had worked so hard to put this thing together, then we should at least put one issue out, and that's exactly what we did.

What was your initial print run?
Five thousand copies.

Where and how did you go about getting those distributed initially?
I had a few other examples of independent publications, so I went to places online where I saw that they were selling, places like Dusty Groove and Turntable Lab. But, for my biggest distribution on that first issue, I went to a company called Fat Beats. Although Fat Beats is primarily known as a record distributor, I saw an opportunity there, so approached them and said, "Maybe while you're out selling records you could offer this magazine as well." The buyer happened to also be a record collector, so he immediately got where we were coming from and took a chance on a small order of a couple hundred copies. He quickly called me about a week or two later saying, "Man, we've completely sold out, do you have any more?" to which I replied, "Yeah, I've got plenty." I just kept shoveling them over to him and as the word got out more retailers started contacting us and eventually I made my way to a real distributor that picked us up for the next few issues.

How does one issue turn to two, three, four, and five? How did you make that happen?
It was a slow process to be honest, because at the time I had no idea about distributors, reserves, advances, and how the whole process of the newsstand works. We were giving them magazines and not understanding that it was probably going to be about six months before we would get any money back.

We had intentions of doing what we called a quarterly magazine journal, so I thought maybe within the next three months we could get the money together, but since we had spent everything to get that first issue out, we had to wait until we collected enough to print the second issue. It took around six months before we could cobble everything together. Once the payments from the distributors and retailers came in we said, "Okay, we have the money now, so let's do a second issue." And remember, at that point, as I said, credit, terms at the printer, and all those types of things were completely foreign to me.

Were you using social media or anything like that back then? As you had a six-month gap, did you have a way of still communicating with or cultivating an audience online?

It's funny you should mention that, because this was literally 2000, so Facebook and Twitter didn't even exist. We had a website but there was very little information up there—it was basically just an "About" page. We weren't even offering magazine subscriptions or direct sale copies from the site at the time. It was really a word-of-mouth type thing and even though it was a niche magazine, what I had discovered online by talking in some of the forums was that the subject matter extended way beyond here in New York and the United States. This was also big in the UK, Germany, Italy, and Japan and eventually we were able to tap into all those international markets, because as we came to find out, they were just as hungry for this type of information as we were.

Okay, I'm smiling because you're actually bringing back memories—I used to be a record collector myself. I remember the buzz of going to all the different record stores trying to find, not specific beats, but "white label" records. They were called Rare Groove, so you would literally have to go everywhere to hunt for certain tracks and when you finally found that piece of vinyl that you'd

been looking for forever it was an amazing feeling. You would pay any amount to have it because you knew that it was a limited edition and hardly anybody else would have it.

Yeah, that's it. Those were the people we were trying to talk to. That's it!

What about social media now? How do you use it to your advantage? I see you have a large rather engaged following over the channels and that's not easy to accomplish.

Over the years we've certainly become more aware of social media's importance. I think we were almost a little bit late to the game—as a print magazine, we never really prioritized it early on. As the web became more of a focus for advertisers we were a little behind the eight ball, just thinking, "Oh well, we're not a website, we're a print magazine." Not understanding at the time that the web was going to swallow everything up. I think once we saw the writing on the wall we began making more of an effort. For us it's really about sharing the right content.

Most of our traffic now comes through Facebook. Two years ago it was Google and people were going to our homepage, but now Facebook dominates search, so it's about that single piece of content that will pull people in, not to your homepage any longer but directly to that piece. So we try to keep it open in a way that our followers can offer up suggestions on both our Facebook and Twitter pages. We try to make sure that we're sharing content we

waxpoetics™

HIP-HOP, JAZZ, FUNK, & SOUL

PARLIAMENT FUNKADELIC

GEORGE CLINTON • BERNIE WORRELL
BOOTSY COLLINS • GARRY SHIDER
BILLY "BASS" NELSON • THE PARLIAMENTS
PEDRO BELL • OVERTON LLOYD

believe is going to work online. It's taken time to get a better understanding of what does and doesn't work, but now we're extremely committed to building up this digital side, especially since all the advertising money has marched out of print.

There were a few years there where people weren't quite sure how things were going to play out online. Everything seems to be standardized now, and aside from your regular banner ads I think the real opportunities are in content marketing and working with brands creating content. Obviously that hinges on your audience size, so we've tried to build that side of the business up as much as we can with the limited resources that we have, and at the same time we're hunting for more resources and partners who can really take the digital side to the next level.

I think what you're saying is that social media can be great in order to attract advertisers, they want to see that you have a strong social media presence, but how does that translate to magazine subscriptions? Do you see any correlation between the two?
I would say that almost by default a lot of people use social media to contact us about their subscriptions, even though there's a completely separate place where they should go for that, but they feel like it's an open forum. When we have a new issue we'll push it through social media and we find that a lot of direct sales come after, and a few subscriptions

on the heels of that. So if there's an issue they're excited about, it may prompt them to take the plunge and jump in for a year or so. But our subscriptions have always remained somewhat marginal to our newsstand and our direct-copy sales so we haven't made it a huge focus.

Being that the price point on the magazine is a little higher than some, it's hard for us to offer a super-discounted subscription—you know, twelve issues for a dollar type thing, like you see with so many other magazines. So we've never used subscriptions as a driver like the big magazines do. They collect as many names and as much information as possible to get circulation numbers that will allow them to increase their rate base to advertisers. They then write off the loss on issue sales, or balance it out, with the increase they receive in ad sales.

We've just made subscriptions something a reader can engage in if they want to, but understanding that a subscription is thirty-two dollars for four issues, it's still somewhat cost-prohibitive for people to just jump in willy-nilly. So yeah, we've tried to make sure that we keep that as an option, but it certainly hasn't been a great focus of ours over the years.

What is your distribution strategy? Do most of your sales come from the web, newsstand, or music stores? What area do you focus on the most?
I've split it up over the years. We definitely do one of the bigger distributors for newsstands,

and that's primarily working with Barnes and Noble in regard to brick-and-mortar locations. There are a few smaller chains throughout the country like Hastings and some other specialty bookstore chains as well. I've remained a close ally with Fat Beats, our first distributor, and they are definitely more on the "mom and pop" record store tip.

While I've maintained this newsstand presence, I've also tried to make sure we've stayed in our niche at the record stores where we first started, even though those are closing down left and right as well, which almost makes it that much more important to make sure that if any do still exist, that they're carrying *Wax Poetics*. That goes for US to international distribution as well.

We started a Japanese version of the magazine so that we might have a better presence over there, knowing there were a lot of Japanese readers who were buying the mag but couldn't understand it. They just liked the way it looked and felt that the content appealed to them photo-wise, but they couldn't really dig into it, so this became a solution to provide them with something they can read. And then we do a smaller percentage of direct sales through our website, which goes directly to consumers. So those three channels probably cover the main ways that we sell copies.

How many people do you have working on the magazine full-time?

It's interesting, because a couple years ago I actually shut down our office. We had offices in Dumbo, Brooklyn and it just got to be so exorbitant that I couldn't rationalize having an office and keeping all these people in there as newsstand sales were continually sliding. So I had to make a decision whether to shut it down as it existed, a full functioning office and magazine, or take it back to how we had started almost—where it was something that we did in conjunction with everything else we were doing.

That was probably one of the hardest decisions I've had to make, but it has really paid off. We were able to streamline things, get it back down to its core, so now it's really just my two partners and me. Most of our contributors are spread out all over the world. My other editor has always lived in San Diego. I have a copy editor in Pennsylvania. My designer is in San Francisco. Sales people would be moving to Las Vegas but still working with us. So it became a situation where it was me and maybe two other people in the office and I was like, "Why do we even have this? Nearly everybody we work with is somewhere else." So that made it a little easier to make a decision.

Due to the web becoming such a huge part of what we need to do now, having an office with a group of interns and having someone who can sit there all day on the web is really what we're focused on now. I've been working on proposals to bring on a few different partners over the last year. So if we do put our energy into building that office back up with a small staff, then the focus wouldn't necessarily be on the print version of the magazine but really on monetizing the digital side.

Once the magazine can exist at the break-even point, I think the real money to be made is online if we can get the money to build that side up. We can keep the print version as a kind of vanity project almost, or as the cornerstone of the brand but not let it be the center of our business plan, which needs to change anyway to become more of an online strategy.

When you say digital, are you talking online or are you talking about monetizing an app?
Definitely talking online. Apps—we have one in the newsstand store so you can get the digital copy of the magazine. We have a partner that builds them and we've talked about an actual stand-alone app, but I think it would probably be something that we did in conjunction with a bigger web presence once that's a little bit more established, which will give us one more platform we can pump content through. I think primarily for us, it's really just the website with paid views and unique visitors. Those two components are primarily what advertisers are looking for, and at this point that's pretty much our bread and butter, so I have to follow where the money goes.

With the music scene so vast, how do you keep up with what's going on and manage to stay abreast of it all in order to remain relevant to your audience?
Well I'm a huge fan of music myself, and a lot of the new music too. As we hit ten, eleven, twelve years old, we understand that there's a new generation of readers coming into the fold. Some of the older readers may not be as receptive to the new sounds but I look at it like any other magazine that's been around for fifty years or so. I mean, *Rolling Stone* isn't still putting Jim Morrison and The Doors on the cover, so at some point you have to turn the page into a new era.

I've certainly tried to make sure that we keep recruiting younger writers who pitch us things they find interesting. I stay open to everything I hear and assign pieces on people I feel are worthy. I also stay open to things my interns may suggest—and some of our writers who've been with us for a long time who've written about older soul and jazz artists might also be interested in up-to-date contemporary music as well. They want to spread their wings a bit so we give them the opportunity to hit both sides of their passion points from the old to the new. What we try to provide is that balance in giving somebody that classic material combined with newer artists who are speaking to that legacy and that particular tradition.

What do you find to be the most challenging about running a magazine?
Wow, there are a number of challenges. Certainly at this point the financial aspects of running

a magazine and dealing with newsstand costs and printing costs and distributor fees, as well as the rising price of paper and oil and shipping costs. Then there's just the state of the newsstand in general. It's been rather frustrating for us not having been in this industry for fifty years like some of these other publications who have really become accustomed to this old model. And just trying to adapt to this new media landscape. We're kind of victims along with everyone else of this kind of apathy amongst other publishers who are larger. Along with this idea that print is dead, they're just sitting, watching the violins play as the Titanic goes down—they really don't have any new ideas on how to change the business model so they're kind of just waiting to ride it on out to retirement.

For us it's like, "Hey, we've only been here thirteen years. I want to do this for another thirty, forty, fifty years. We can't just let this die here." So I've been working voraciously with Ingram and other distributors to try and figure out a new model that may work. Something like print on demand is something I'm very interested in now, trying to see if there's a way we can adapt that model to the current newsstand system. There are a few hurdles in getting that to work, but I think that the newsstand pressures and the general state of magazines are a huge challenge right now for anybody who's doing print.

Advertising and this online animal is another challenge that we're still dealing with—trying to get a large enough audience that will appeal to advertisers but doing it in a way that doesn't compromise our original vision and turn off our core audience in lieu of finding a bigger group of people. So those are the two biggest challenges that I face right now.

What do you find most rewarding about running a magazine?
For me, it's the challenge. I look at it like—I mean, I got my degree in painting and I look at this as my ultimate art project, because with a painting you start working on it and once it's done you hang it on the wall somewhere and move on. It's a similar process for me in the way that I put issues together, where I have a very broad idea and a few specifics on what will fit into this idea or theme, but as I start working on it there's a lot of painting over and smudging out to do and so forth. It starts out with a whole bunch of ideas and over the course of two or three months it whittles down into this one set of articles that becomes something that will exist in physical form in perpetuity. And then just like a painting, it goes on the wall and I can't touch it anymore.

That process of the back-and-forth and the challenge of overcoming obstacles with PR people or management or record labels in order to get the pieces in and on time—that process is what keeps me going and invigorated. Trying to continuously challenge, not only myself, but my audience as well. I'm still growing as an individual and I'm well aware that we're always growing as a business too.

WP

Wax Poetics
10th Anniversary
WINTER 2012
Issue 50

Prince

I want to make sure that I'm still having fun doing this. I want to keep my readers on their toes. I want to keep myself on my toes and try to do things that I haven't done before, exploring new types of music, new areas, and new artists. That process is what keeps me going and keeps me interested in this enough that I'll forgo hours of sleep in order to make it all happen.

From your experience, what factors do you think contribute to the success of a magazine in general?

I definitely think establishing a connection with your audience. We've set out to provide a consistent idea over the last thirteen years. I set a bar early on that we never really wanted to go any lower than, and I've just wanted to keep raising that bar over the years.

I think in order to keep people coming back and keep coming out of pocket you need to be delivering consistently on the promise that you made to your audience. Delivering on the kinds of things that they're going to find interesting and challenging in a way that reflects their growth as individuals too.

I am very aware that when we started the magazine some of our readers were late teens, early twenties, and they're now in their thirties and forties, so they are not the same people. They were running around and doing whatever ten, thirteen years ago and now some are married, some have children, and some have mortgages.

Their lives have changed, the way they feel about music has changed and grown, and I think it's important to show that you're doing that as a publication as well. Then at the same time keeping your eye on the next generation and bringing them into the fold and making them part of the vision so that it continues to grow, decade after decade.

Would you say it's the opposite of that that contributes to a magazine's failure?

I would. A lot of what I've seen, even personally in dealing with magazines that I loved at one point, is that sometimes the ones that don't make it are the ones that have compromised their integrity. I think people are looking for something real in this world, something they can connect to, and when they feel betrayed because a magazine suddenly decided to throw all its initial mission out the window in pursuit of more money, more advertisers, and a bigger audience, I think the audience can see that taking place and it turns off many a reader from countless magazines.

Even for myself, magazines I thought I would love forever, all of a sudden they were just no longer the same. I understand the growing pains and frustrations in trying to get there without such a huge compromise, it's a tightrope you need to walk. It's one that we've tried to tiptoe down instead of charging like a bull in a china shop and causing too much havoc early on. I've tried to do it incrementally almost, so the change was not so evident and stark. It was more of an ease-in over a year or a few issues that set it up so it wasn't as jarring, in maybe covering a certain artist or type of music that a reader may not be as interested in, or at least they don't think they are. I put myself in the position of trying to provide them with things I think they should know about. That's been the mission from day one, trying to keep people open-minded more than anything else, and we want to continue doing that.

How do you handle ad sales? What type of advertisers do you typically go after? I presume you have a specific type for your niche audience.

Well, we appeal to music lovers who are primarily male. If you look at our demographic, they're right in the ideal bracket for advertisers—in that eighteen- to thirty-five-year-old range. Knowing what we do, we see where these advertisers remain committed in other magazines, or it could be relationships we've had with certain sneaker companies like Adidas or Converse who remain committed to the music space and are doing interesting things.

Unfortunately, a lot of our advertisers, from say maybe five years ago, have gone out of business now because they were primarily small record labels and stores who suffered tremendously after the Great Recession. So we've had to adjust and understand that while those advertisers may be falling by the wayside, we're looking at the Toyotas of the world who are trying to appeal to a more traditional African American audience, so we can kind of balance some of the loss from the smaller labels and stores with the bigger ads we receive from the Fortune 500 companies.

We've always tried to maintain that balance between the two, to give it that sense of authenticity rather than just going after a bunch of corporate advertisers and not really caring about the little guys. We'll cut better deals for the guys who don't have as much money, knowing that we're going to be able to balance that out with some of the bigger advertising brands.

What is your current circulation?

About fifty-five to sixty thousand, somewhere in there.

At what point were you able to go after some of the bigger advertisers?

I think probably in the twenty to thirty thousand range was when we started to pick up steam. We were probably closer to seventy, seventy-five thousand a few years ago, but as the newsstand started to decrease I've adjusted our numbers to make sure that we stay in the right range and are not overshooting the mark. I think once you get to a certain level you pop up on the radar of some of the agencies, because the brands themselves always have that intermediary agency that you're forced to deal with.

While the guy at the brand may love your magazine, there's going to be a guy at the

waxpoetics

agency who's not concerned with the love because he's really all about the numbers—do you have them and can you deliver on the audience that you're promising? Again, it's one of those tightropes we walk in trying to make sure that we appeal to both the business interest of the agency and the passion points of the brand and present them with something that makes sense for them.

I'm interested in keeping those relationships continuing instead of it just being a one shot thing where they're in and out. I'd like there to be something we can build on and eventually turn into something beyond a one- or two-page ad in the magazine, something more that goes into creating content, an event series or something like that, where we can go beyond just the book advertising into a lot of the more profitable ways of working with brands.

What would you say are important skills or disciplines that a magazine publisher would need today?
I think patience certainly, because one thing about this is that it never moves quite as quickly as you want it to. Even the process of getting an issue together is very time-consuming and goes through a lot of twists and turns, while you want things to change quickly. For instance, I had an idea about something I wanted to do in the magazine, which took almost a year before I was able to actually see it fully realized in print. So it requires that you have a very long-term vision for things, knowing that by the time you start working on something the world isn't going to get a chance to see it for maybe two, three, four months after.

I think staying a step ahead and being patient and always thinking into the future, because by the time a magazine issue comes out, I get it, I flip through it, but it's really old hat to me. I worked on it three months prior for three or four months, I've read all the articles a million times—it looks great, everything's fine, but I'm already on to the next thing. So I think that sense of living in the future is something that serves publishers well. Not getting too caught up in the now and how everything is at this very moment.

Do you have a last message of wisdom or inspiration for readers who maybe considering launching a publication themselves?
I wish you all the best first of all, because it's certainly not easy. But I definitely think there's still a place for print magazines. I think what we're seeing now is a backlash from the print-is-dead movement. I'm running into a lot of younger twenty-something-year-olds who are interested in making physical magazines.

I think there is something on the horizon that's going to be like the internet of things, where print magazines will be very tied into what is coming on and off the internet. It's important for a publisher to understand print within the larger world of media and the value that it holds. You need to understand what your publication means to your audience and stay true to that vision, which is a challenge, especially as things are constantly shifting and changing in the media landscape underneath us. Try to stick to your guns and not compromise your vision in lieu of a greater—or what seemingly may seem like a greater—opportunity. It can be so easy to inadvertently pull your eyes off the prize, that's why I think that staying true to your vision is of the utmost importance.

Finally, is there anything else that you'd like to add or wish I'd asked?
Hmm, that's interesting. In regard to the mechanics of publishing a magazine, what I've seen in dealing with a lot of people who've gone to college for journalism is that they get trained and they know all the technical terms to talk about magazines and what they mean, but sometimes that knowledge becomes a huge barrier to unleashing their creative energies. I think the naïveté that I had going into this certainly served me well, and knowing some of the things that I shouldn't do early on maybe would've saved me time and money, but they were huge growing periods for us in under-standing how this all works. I think if I had known too much about this industry and the way it all worked I probably would never have started. So there is something to be said for really just following your passion and your heart and doing something that makes you feel good and not overthinking things to the point of thinking your way out of an idea.

OUTRO

I only hope that you have enjoyed reading these interviews as much as I enjoyed conducting them. The reason I asked all the publishers essentially the same questions (although I did divert as necessary) was to give a good basis for understanding how each of them handled specific scenarios or situations. If you decide to take just one idea from each chapter, then you already have sixteen ideas that you can start to build into some type of plan—and that was exactly my purpose in putting this all together.

After speaking with these publishers, I came to realize that although the subject is often called "mass communication," I truly believe that we are past that point and into a time where everything is becoming more specialized, personalized, and individualized—so why shouldn't those factors also apply to magazines? With so many people who have so many different interests, hobbies, wants, and needs, why does a magazine have to sell two hundred thousand copies in order for it to be considered successful?

It's evident to me that as these publishers seek to find the sweet spot for delivering content over the mediums of print, web, digital, and social media, the magazine business model as it currently exists is not only obsolescent, but obsolete. These publishers are risking it all, tenaciously persevering as they continue to innovate and experiment while on a mission that is often bigger than "self" (some are not even operating at profit) that they might pave the way in creating new models that are more conducive to the dissemination of information according to our most current media consumption habits.

Dare I say that the days of "mass communication" are over, and that's why if you have an idea and a smart plan—and have considered everything these publishers have said—then just *maybe* you should go for it. But remember, as Michael Brooke of *Concrete Wave* said, "Don't publish a magazine, document a movement!"

GLOSSARY

Ad sales rep: Person responsible for calling and setting up appointments with advertisers; in charge of maintaining current accounts and generating new business.

Advertising director: Manages a staff of ad sales representatives; responsible for generating advertising in magazine through direct selling and promotional activities.

Affidavit of returns: A statement of returns that shows how many copies of a magazine were not sold through a particular distribution outlet.

Agreement: A negotiated and legally binding arrangement, or document, between two parties.

Alignment: The position of text on a page; can be left, right, centered, or justified.

Allotment: The number of magazines a publisher sends to a distributor, wholesaler, or retailer.

Ancillary products: A product or service a publisher can sell in addition to the magazine to extend their brand and generate additional income. Examples include hats, pens, bags, T-shirts, seminars, audio books, and other promotional items.

Aqueous coating: A clear, shiny, water-based coating which is applied like ink by a printing press.

Art director: Oversees the artistic design of the magazine and works closely with the editorial director to ensure that the design is consistent with the editorial philosophy.

Article: A piece of writing included in a magazine.

Artwork: Visual materials such as photographs or illustrations.

Associate editor: A staff editorial person who supports and assists the editor with writing, editing, and assigning material as required. May also be responsible for writing titles, subtitles, and captions.

Audit bureau: An organization that audits and verifies publishers' claimed circulation numbers. Advertisers then use these official reports. Reputable auditing companies include BPA Worldwide and the Audit Bureau of Circulations (ABC).

Bar code: Also known as a Universal Product Code, or UPC. It is a unique fourteen-digit number that allows retailers to track the sales of a magazine through computerized inventory control systems; provides information such as the magazine name, issue number, price, inventory available, and date the magazine should be removed from the racks.

Binding: A method of attaching pages together in a magazine; can be either saddle-stitched or perfect bound.

Bipad: The five-digit number contained in a magazine's barcode that uniquely identifies the magazine's title for the life of the magazine.

Bitmap images: Images that are created using a grid of individual pixels that are each assigned a different color or shade. Example formats include bmp, tiff, gif, and jpeg files.

Bleed: Artwork or color that extends off the edge of the page after trimming.

Blow-in: Method of inserting unattached cards between the pages of a magazine.

Body copy: The main text of a story.

Body type: The font used for body copy.

Book: Term used to describe a magazine.

Brand: The specific and unique identity of a business, product, service, or concept.

Business manager: Supervises internal office management.

Business reply mail (BRM) service: A direct response vehicle that is used by businesses, publishers, government departments, and other organizations to seek responses from recipients within the US (Domestic Business Reply Mail) or from recipients around the world (International Business Reply Mail).

Byline: A particular author's name and brief biographical information that accompanies an article.

Callout: Text from an article that visually breaks up a page and draws a readers' attention.

Caption: Text that identifies a picture or image.

Center alignment: Where text is centered on a page leaving the same sized margin on either sides.

Circulation: The number of readers a particular publication has, calculated through the sum of single copy and subscription sales.

CMYK (4 color, four color, full color, or process color): The four ink colors used for magazine printing: cyan (blue), magenta (red), yellow, and black. The four inks are combined in different quantities to reproduce and print (almost) all colors.

Coated paper: Chemically treated paper that has a glossy, shiny look to it.

Color correct: To adjust the processed colors in order to achieve the desired results.

Column: Usually written by an expert, famous, or respected individual. A column provides credibility for the magazine and is usually written by the same person every month.

Collate: To organize a set of individual sheets or signatures into the proper sequence for binding.

Consumer magazine: General or special interest magazine that is marketed to the public, usually available via newsstand or subscription, and more often than not contains advertising. The main purpose of these types of magazines is to entertain, sell products, and promote viewpoints. Examples include *Readers Digest* and *O Magazine*.

Contributing editors: Writers who are experts in the field that the magazine covers. Regular freelance writers with whom the magazine wishes to maintain a relationship may also be given this title.

Copy editor: Copy editors are not proofreaders. They check written material in its original form (before layout and design), looking for and correcting errors in grammar, spelling, usage, and style. They also check articles for form, length, and completeness.

Copyright: Protects original works of authorship from use without permission.

Copyright infringement: The unauthorized use of a copyrighted work, in whole or in part, without the copyright owner's permission.

Cost per thousand readers (CPM): The measurement of how much money it costs an advertiser to reach 1,000 readers. This amount is calculated by dividing the page price by the number of copies in circulation. If you have 5,000 readers and charge $1,000 per page, then the CPM = $1,000/5 = $200.

Cover line: The short title or teaser that appears on the cover of a magazine.

Crop marks: Printed lines that show where a printed sheet should be trimmed.

Cropping: Cutting away parts of an image that are not required.

Defamation of character: Can include libel, slander, or both.

Demographics: Statistical data relating to a particular group within the population, can include information such as age, income, and education level.

Department: The part of the magazine that a reader becomes familiar with and expects to see in every issue; offers consistency and establishes the tone and voice of your publication. A different contributor may write a department every month. They are grouped together under one common topic so an individual department may have one or several articles.

Draw: See *Allotment*.

Dummy: Mock version of the magazine that demonstrates how the final printed piece will look.

Distributor: A company that represents and sells a catalog of magazine titles to various retail outlets.

Edit: To modify or correct an article.

Editorial assistant: An entry-level employee who supports the more senior editors by performing duties such as researching information, setting up interviews, returning calls, making copies, and filing.

Editorial calendar: A schedule of upcoming editorial content to be featured in upcoming issues. It is used by advertisers to determine what issues may offer product tie-ins according to the planned theme and content.

Editorial director: Person responsible for all final editorial decisions and for managing and coordinating the creative staff to ensure that the publication's editorial philosophy is executed and fulfilled with each issue.

Editorial formula: Describes the actual make-up of the magazine, answering questions like: What is the frequency of the publication? Price? Subscription price? Number of pages? Advertising-to-editorial ratio? Number of columns? Number of departments? Number of features? Etc.

Editorial philosophy: Describes the magazine's main focus and reason for being.

Executive editor: Reports directly to the editor in chief; performs both managerial and editorial duties, keeping the magazine on schedule by enforcing strict deadlines.

Fact checker: Researches submitted articles and checks that the information presented is accurate.

Fair use: Allows for the limited use of copyrighted material without the need for the author's permission or attribution.

Feature: These are the longer articles in a magazine, usually four to six pages in length. They are unique to each issue and most clearly exhibit the magazine's concept.

Finish: The surface appearance of paper, examples include matte and gloss.

First serial rights: Grants the publisher the right to print an article for the first time before anyone else, but all other rights are retained by the author.

Freelancer: Person who sells or contracts their work to many different clients rather than actually being employed by one particular company.

Flatplan: Used to plan and organize the layout and order of pages for publications such as magazines, newspapers, catalogues, and books. Flat plans originally started as drawn out pieces of paper that were stuck to a wall to show the order of articles and advertisements in a publication. As pages were moved or ads were cancelled, the pieces of paper could easily be moved around, annotated, or amended. Paper flatplans are being replaced by digital flatplans, many of which are able to sync with applications such as Adobe InDesign.

Font: A particular typeface, including upper and lower case letters, numbers, punctuation, and special characters.

Four color: See *CMYK*.

Frequency: The number of times a year a magazine is published.

Frequency discount: A reduced advertising rate based upon the number of times an ad is placed in a magazine within a specified period of time.

Graphic designer: Responsible for how the magazine looks. A designer utilizes color, type, illustration, photography, and various print and layout techniques to create a design that effectively communicates and appeals to its intended audience.

Gutter: The white space formed by the two inner margins of the facing pages in a magazine.

Headline: An article's title, which acts as the attention-grabber for a story.

House sheets: Paper that is kept in stock by a printer and is therefore usually cheaper to print on.

Illustration: A drawing or sketch.

Insert: A piece that is prepared for insertion into a magazine such as a subscriptions card.

International Standard Serial Number (ISSN): A unique eight-digit number assigned to a serial publication that is necessary when working with or selling subscriptions to libraries. The number uniquely identifies the title regardless of language or country where it is published.

Justification: Positioning of text so that both the left and right margins appear in a straight line down the sides of a page.

Kerning: Adjusting the space between pairs of letters for a better fit.

Kill fee: The amount paid when a writer has been contracted to write an article but the article is never published.

Lacquer: Clear, shiny coating that is applied to a printed piece for protection.

Layout: The way in which text and pictures are arranged on a page.

Leading: The space between the lines of type on a printed page.

Left alignment: Where text along the left margin appears in a straight line down the page, but the right margin is ragged or misaligned.

Libel: A published false statement that is damaging to a person's reputation, a business, or a product.

Logo: A distinguishing mark, emblem, or symbol that is used to identify a particular organization.

Margin: The edge or border of a page.

Marketing director: Individual responsible for the publicity and promotion of a magazine.

Media kit: Magazine promotional tool consisting of information on a magazine and can include the audience demographics, psychographics, market analysis, circulation numbers, editorial calendar, and advertising rates.

Mockup: See *Dummy*.

Mission statement: Statement that explains a company's aims, values, and reason for being.

Native file: The default file format which works with an application during the creation, edition, or publication of a file. For instance, a Microsoft Excel's .xlsx file is native to Microsoft Excel.

Niche market: A narrowly defined group of potential customers for a magazine's particular subject matter.

One-time rights: When the publisher can publish the article one time, but the writer retains the right to simultaneously sell it elsewhere.

Orphan: Undesirable text formatting where a word or a short sentence appears by itself at either the end of a paragraph, a column, or the bottom of a page.

Other magazines: Magazines that cannot be defined as either consumer or trade.

Overrun: The number of magazines printed in excess of the quantity ordered.

Page count: The total number of pages in a magazine.

Pagination: The process of arranging the sequence of numbers assigned to the pages in a periodical.

Perfect bound: Book binding method where printed pages are shaved along the side and glued at the spine.

Perforate: To pierce or make holes in a printed piece.

Periodical: A publication that is published at regular intervals.

Photo editor: Person responsible for the visuals and images for a magazine's stories. This person can also be tasked with maintaining, cataloging, and storing images.

Plagiarism: Using someone else's work or ideas without acknowledgement and falsely claiming authorship of those works.

Plus cover: A cover that is on a different paper than the inside. In this case, the printing process for the cover would be different from the printing process for the pages that appear on the inside.

Point: The unit of measurement used to describe the size of type and leading. There are seventy-two points in an inch.

Preflight: A software feature that helps package all the elements that a printer needs so the files can be accurately reproduced; includes fonts, pictures, and illustrations.

Premium position: Prime advertising position within a magazine that is sold at a higher rate. Positions include the inside front cover, inside back cover, back outer cover, or center spread.

Prepress: The process of getting a document ready for print.

Press release: A public announcement prepared for distribution to various news media outlets.

Printer: Vendor responsible for manufacturing the final product, printing, and binding the magazine.

Process color: See *CMYK*.

Production director: Creates, coordinates, and oversees the production schedule to ensure the magazine is produced on time. Can help staff members format material so all pages are complete and technically accurate. May also oversee the magazine's press run.

Production schedule: A plan or timetable that describes the workflow, tasks, and deadlines necessary to ensure that a magazine is produced on time.

Promotions director: See *Marketing director.*

Proof: A copy of the actual magazine that is used to check for errors and flaws in order to make corrections before the final piece is printed.

Proofreader: Checks over the final proof for typographical and mechanical errors.

Psychographics: The study and classification of people according to their attitudes, aspirations, values, beliefs, and other psychological criteria.

Public relations (PR): Activities undertaken by a company or individual to protect, enhance, or build their reputation through the use of various media outlets and mediums.

Publication: A book, magazine, newspaper, journal, or musical piece that is offered for sale.

Publisher: Oversees the business side of the magazine and is ultimately responsible for the magazine's profitability. Duties include budgeting, strategic planning, and ad development.

Pull quote: A quote—usually not more than a sentence or two—that is extracted from the main text of an article and set off from other information on the page using lines, shading, or boxes.

Query letter: Introductory letter to an editor that describes the idea for an article that an author would like to submit.

Rate card: Summarizes a publisher's prices for ads of different sizes, colors, and positions. Also summarizes the frequency discounts for consecutive ads being placed in the magazine.

Resolution: Indicates the number of dots per inch and refers to the sharpness of an image.

RGB: The primary additive colors of red, green, and blue. When these colors are combined equally, they produce white, and when they are combined in different amounts, they can produce a broad array of colors. TV and computer monitors produce images using the RGB method.

Right alignment: Where text along the right margin appears in a straight line down the page, but the left margin is ragged or misaligned.

Rights-managed stock photography: A photo (or illustration) that is licensed for one-time, specific use only.

Royalty-free stock photography: Allows for the unlimited use of a photo (or illustration) in any media as defined by the licensing agreement.

Saddle stitch: Book binding method where magazine leaves are secured through the centerfold by wire staples.

Sans serif: Fonts that are straight and have no serifs or curlicues at the end of the letters—generally used for headlines, sub-heads, and sidebars.

Scaling: Enlarging or reducing the size of an image.

Score: To crease paper along a straight line so it can be folded accurately.

Second serial (reprint) rights: A nonexclusive license that gives the publication the right to publish a story, article, or poem after another periodical has already published the piece.

Self-cover: A magazine cover that is printed on the same paper stock as found on the inside.

Sell-through rate: The percentage of magazines sent to distributors that are actually sold.

Serif: Fonts that have curlicues at the end of the letters, which make them easier to read and is generally used for body text.

Senior editor: Writes, edits, proofreads, and copy-edits articles; helps assign articles to writers, making sure they understand the specifics. Other names for this title include feature editor, beauty editor, fashion editor, and so forth.

Sheet-fed press: A printing press that prints on individual sheets of paper as opposed to rolls. This method is much slower and more expensive than using a web press.

Shipping galley: A list that a distributor provides that shows the name, address, and the number of magazines ordered by a wholesaler or retailer.

Sidebar: A short piece of text placed alongside a main article that is typically boxed off and contains additional or explanatory information.

Signature: A printed sheet that has been folded at least once and will become part of a magazine.

Single-copy sales: Magazines that are sold through a website, retail outlet, or an event.

Slander: A false spoken statement that is damaging to a person's reputation, a business, or a product.

Spread: Two facing pages with an even-numbered page on the left and an odd-numbered page on the right.

Spot color: A specially mixed ink that is applied individually on the printing press as opposed to a mix of the four (CMYK) inks which make up process printing. The most popular company that makes spot colors is Pantone, Inc. They sell color guides (or swatch books) that enable printers to mix and create the exact same colors from a set of base inks.

Staff writer: Resident staff member who writes and contributes articles to the magazine.

Stock photography: Ready-made images available for download online.

Style guide: A written set of standards or rules that should be followed when either writing or designing documents for a specific publication, organization, or field.

Subscriptions card: The mail piece that appears inside a magazine that makes it easy for readers to subscribe.

Tracking: The process of adjusting the amount of space between the words on a page.

Trade magazines: Trade magazines are business-to-business magazines. Their audience consists of readers in a particular trade or profession. Although some may be available on newsstands (e.g., *ComputerUser*, *Communication Arts*, etc.), most are sold through subscription only. Examples include *AJN: American Journal of Nursing* and *Cognitive Psychology*.

Trademark: A distinctive word, name, mark, emblem, or symbol that is legally registered to identify the goods made or sold by a person or entity, and differentiates them from the goods made or sold by another person or entity. Trademarks grant exclusive rights to the owner that prevent competitors from using similar marks in the marketplace.

Trim size: The final page size or dimensions of a magazine after it has been trimmed.

Typeface: See *Font*.

Typography: The art of setting and arranging type on a page.

Uncoated paper: Untreated paper.

Underrun: The number of printed magazines delivered that is less than the quantity ordered.

UV coating: A high gloss, heavy coating that is applied to a printed piece or magazine cover. It is more expensive and durable than varnish coating.

Varnish: Clear, shiny coating that is applied to a printed piece for protection. Varnish is not as heavy or shiny as UV coating but is a cheaper alternative.

Vector graphic: A type of computer graphic created using mathematical formulas that can be enlarged or reduced without any loss of quality.

Viral marketing tools: Tools that make it easy for a visitor to share information about a site, company, product, or event etc. (also known as "word-of-mouth marketing").

Web press: A printing press that prints both sides simultaneously on large, continuous rolls of paper that are then cut into sheets after printing.

Web statistics: Tracks the number of visitors to a website and analyzes behavior, providing information on where visitors came from, what day and time they visited, how long they spent, what path they took, and other statistical information.

Website editor: Responsible for creating and editing web content.

Widow: Undesirable text formatting where a paragraph ending line appears by itself at the top of the following page (or column) and is therefore separated from the rest of the text.

Wholesalers: Companies that work on behalf of publishers to distribute and deliver magazine titles to specific territories and retail stores.

Word spacing: The amount of space between words.

Work for hire: Where a copyright is transferred from an employee to the employer that the work was originally created for.

ABOUT THE AUTHOR

Lorraine Phillips attended Jackson State University, where she received an MBA in business administration and a BS in computer science, graduating both programs with honors and distinction. She later went on to earn an AA in graphic design from Bauder College and was elected to Who's Who Among Students in American Universities & Colleges for outstanding merit and accomplishments.

Lorraine, former publisher of *SisterPower Magazine*, is a creative information technology professional with over fourteen years' experience in planning, developing, and publishing print, internet, and digital projects. She has published six books, with subjects ranging from personal motivation to magazine publishing to online marketing and promotion.

As an author Lorraine has received several awards. Her books have been recognized for exhibiting superior levels of creativity and originality as well as high standards of design and production quality. She was also selected for what is one of the country's most respected book awards, being named a Benjamin Franklin Awards silver finalist in the Business and Economics category for excellence in book editorial and design.

Lorraine is currently a freelance user experience designer. As a dynamic speaker, author, freelancer, and coach, it is her mission to help people achieve their personal and professional dreams. As she puts it in her own words, "It's exactly what I was born to do!"

BY
THIS
AUTHOR

Magazine Business Plan Kit

If you're seriously thinking about publishing a magazine, then it's a good idea to start with a plan. This sample magazine business plan kit will help you map out and strategize the future of your magazine, estimate start-up and ongoing costs, outline the resources you will need, set measurable goals and objectives so you always know where you stand, evaluate and study the competition, understand your markets and how best to satisfy them, raise funds or attract investors, and most importantly, determine whether your business model can function at a profit. To find out more, please visit soipublishedamag.com.

Publish Your First Magazine (Second Edition): A Practical Guide for Wannabe Publishers

Lorraine Phillips, former publisher of *SisterPower Magazine*, went from idea to newsstand after landing three distribution deals on her first attempt and has now created a practical guide for potential publishers that demonstrates her process and provides the details on exactly how she did it. This new and expanded edition covers such topics as magazine business fundamentals, how to brand and design a publication, how to manage the editorial process, the necessary start-up costs, the different ways a magazine can be monetized, the legalities of publishing, and much more. Now you can learn in a weekend what took this author two years to research—it's exactly what's needed for anyone who's contemplating producing a print magazine in today's highly volatile and competitive marketplace. For more, please visit publishyourfirstmagazine.com.

Publish Your First Digital Magazine: Taking You from Concept to Delivery

If you're serious about publishing a digital magazine, then look no further. *Publish Your First Digital Magazine* is a must-read for all creatives who are passionate about sharing a message with their audience and looking for innovative ideas, strategies, tools, and techniques they can use to do so. Covering flip books, apps, online newsstands, and blog-style magazines, you will learn how to create an editorial philosophy, how to build an editorial calendar, where to find content and images, various ways a digital magazine can be monetized, and how to effectively use social media to connect with your audience. For more, please visit firstdigitalmagazine.com.

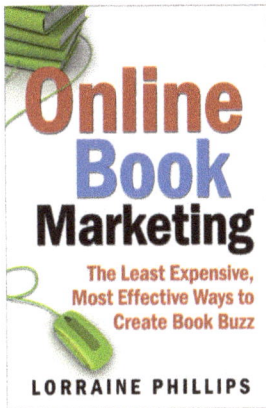

Online Book Marketing:
The Least Expensive, Most Effective Ways to Create Book Buzz

If you're an author or publisher who really wants to sell books, then you've got to create a platform that will connect, communicate, and build long-term relationships with your readers online. *Online Book Marketing* will show you how, providing you with ideas and strategies you can use to effectively brand and promote your book on the internet almost entirely for FREE. You will learn how to effectively use Twitter, Facebook, LinkedIn, and YouTube; methods for engaging readers through articles, newsletters, audio podcasts, and videos; ways to drive targeted traffic to your website or blog; and how to use search engine optimization (SEO) techniques that will increase your visibility on the web. For more, please visit onlinebookbuzz.com.

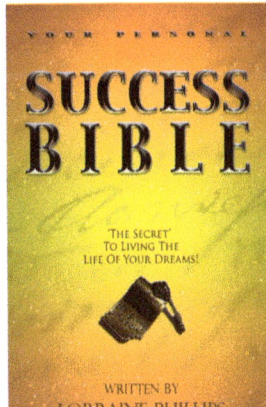

Your Personal Success Bible:
'The Secret' to Living the Life of Your Dreams!

If you want more out of life, have failed to achieve some of the results you would like, are not doing some of the things you know you should, or are just not sure which direction to take, then this is the book for you. In *Your Personal Success Bible* Lorraine Phillips leads readers on a journey of introspection and self-discovery in a way that allows them to become fully motivated and able to unlock and achieve their full potential. In rather simple, layman terms, Phillips takes the law of attraction and makes it more logical and adaptable by providing an updated view that includes some of the latest developments in both psychology and neuroscience. For more, please visit yourpersonalsuccessbible.com.

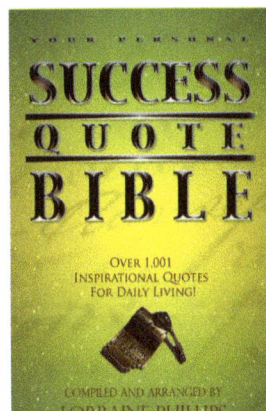

Your Personal Success Quote Bible:
Over 1,001 Inspirational Quotes for Daily Living!

This remarkable collection of insightful, uplifting, and thought-provoking words of wisdom will prove to be an invaluable tool for you on your journey to success. Created to keep you motivated and inspired, you will find quotes from Napoleon Hill, Socrates, Buddha, William Shakespeare, Tupac Shakur, Lao Tzu, Albert Einstein, Confucius, Bob Marley, and Plato, just to name a few. In addition, the book is divided into more than fifty relevant "daily living" categories, such as abundance and wealth, attitude, dreams and imagination, faith, forgiveness, gratitude, and love and relationships. With its complete index of authors, this compilation will prove to be a quick and easy, user-friendly guide where you'll always be able to find the perfect quote! For more, please visit yourpersonalsuccessbible.com/products.htm.

www.ingramcontent.com/pod-product-compliance
Lightning Source LLC
Chambersburg PA
CBHW050105220326
41598CB00043B/7386